LIVING WITH ANGELS

Bringing angels into your everyday life

angel blessings
to
Niki
from
theolyn

LIVING WITH ANGELS

ANGELS

Bringing angels into your everyday life

THEOLYN CORTENS

PIATKUS

Copyright © 2003 by Theolyn Cortens

First published in 2003 by
Piatkus Books Ltd
5 Windmill Street
London W1T 2JA
e-mail: info@piatkus.co.uk

This edition published in 2004
Reprinted in 2005
The moral right of the author has been asserted

*A catalogue record for this book is available
from the British Library*

ISBN 0 7499 2565 5

Edited by Jan Cutler
Text design by Briony Chappell, Goldust Design

This book has been printed on paper manufactured
with respect for the environment using wood from
managed sustainable resources

Typeset by Phoenix Photosetting, Chatham, Kent
Printed and bound in Great Britain by Bookmarque Ltd, Croydon, Surrey

Dedication

For my husband, life companion and soulmate, Will

Contents

Acknowledgements   ix

Introduction   1

1 WHO ARE THE ANGELS?   9
2 ANGELS THROUGH HISTORY   27
3 ANGELS IN MODERN TIMES   41
4 PREPARING TO MEET THE ANGELS   55
5 MEETING YOUR GUARDIAN ANGEL   77
6 MANIFESTING ABUNDANCE   95
7 CO-CREATION   117
8 ANGELS WITH A PURPOSE   131
9 THE ARCHANGELS OF THE ZODIAC   145
10 THE ARCHANGELS OF THE TREE OF LIFE   161

A Farewell Blessing   183
Appendix: Angelic Symbols   185
Resources   191
Soul School Courses   197

Index   199

Acknowledgements

A special thank you to Anthea for her help in bringing this book into the world. Blessings to all the loving people in my life who have encouraged and supported me. And thank you to my angels and guides for their messages of joy and delight.

Material on page 45 is summarised with permission of Bantam Books. Material on page 49 is summarised with permission of Blake Publishing.

Introduction

Angels can fly because they take themselves lightly.

G. K. CHESTERTON

I have been working with angels for over 30 years, and during this period the public interest in angels has steadily increased. For some time I have been sharing my experiences with others through lectures and workshops; now, through this book, I hope to help more people to bring angels into their lives. In it I shall be introducing you to the hidden magic of the angelic worlds, where all things are possible, and will be helping you to communicate and work with angels of many kinds. There is nothing new about communicating with angels; throughout history, from ancient times and in many cultures, there are records of intelligent, compassionate beings, who come from invisible realms to help, console, or bring messages of hope. Today, in our busy, stressful and materialistic world, angels are becoming increasingly popular – they even feature regularly in novels and films. More and more ordinary, often sceptical people are describing angelic encounters. There are stories of people being rescued when lost on a moor or mountain by a stranger who then vanishes into thin air. Others have heard a voice from nowhere warning of impending danger, or felt an invisible hand gently push them out of the way of an oncoming lorry.

At the same time, an increasing number of people are reaching out towards the angels, seeking their help and support, and getting it –

for example in difficult circumstances, such as a family illness or personal crisis. Healers and therapists are often assisted by angelic presences. (And quite a few drivers find that calling on a 'parking angel' actually helps them to find a parking space! There are plenty of everyday angels for minor tasks.) We are no longer waiting for angels to visit us; more and more people are seeking active communication with these beings of light, often by attending workshops and courses given by people like myself, for whom angels are a part of daily life.

How I Came to Work with the Angels

I spent my childhood in a remote part of the Cotswolds in England. There were hardly any cars in those days and the peaceful, unpolluted countryside seemed magical. I was always aware of something buzzing, a creative energy urging the flowers and trees to grow. When I first heard of fairies I was determined to meet them; on moonlit nights I would watch from my bedroom window, in the hope of seeing them dancing. I never did, but I knew for certain they were there. And on clear nights, I could sense the stars singing to me.

My parents followed no religious practices – my stepfather, indeed, was a total sceptic. The first person to introduce me to spiritual ideas was my aunt, who was a theosophist and an amateur astrologer. I used to go and stay with her, and discovered her stock of fascinating books, which I read eagerly. From them I learned that all natural things – human beings, trees, flowers, even stars – are protected and guided by angels or spirits. According to theosophy the natural world is full of spirits; the fairies I longed to see are nature spirits, who busily maintain the nature kingdom that humans depend on.

Theosophy is a mystical religion that brings together ideas from Eastern religions and Western philosophies. My aunt's books explained that all religions are based on the same sacred truth: that the world we live in is created by a divine intelligence or power, which is benevolent and compassionate. All the great teachers and prophets throughout history have taught the same timeless wisdom, which has developed in different ways according to cultural and historical needs. Theosophy also speaks of the journey of the soul through many lifetimes as it evolves and grows in wisdom.

There was no Bible in our house, but when I was nine I came across one of the most beautiful pieces of biblical writing, the Song of Solomon, in a poetry book of my mother's. This wonderful hymn of praise to the Creator awoke in me a sense of my spiritual being, and I developed a thirst for something that the humanist approach to life did not offer. At the age of 14 I joined the Buddhist Society, and from then on I was on the hunt for the perfect religion. Over time I tried several different spiritual paths: Buddhism followed by Christianity and then transcendental meditation. I never became a theosophist, though I read more of the literature, and found the philosophy of a deep truth contained in all religions very much in tune with my own beliefs. But it was after I learned to meditate that my visions began.

A New Beginning

I have never forgotten my first angelic experience and how it changed my whole approach to life.

In 1974, as I approached my thirtieth birthday, I was physically and mentally depleted. For the last ten years I had been bringing up two children on my own (their father had gone to live abroad). I was living near my parents in Durham, where I had just completed a teacher-training course; I was exhausted, and it is not surprising that I fell ill with a nasty dose of mumps, as well as developing asthma. To help my healing process I spent a lot of time in bed, meditating. Sometimes I felt very sad and lonely, overwhelmed by the stress of my life as a single mother; at these times I would pray in order to help myself feel more secure.

One day I began to get a strong feeling that something special was going to happen, a feeling that became more and more powerful over the next few days. Finally, one morning, when I was feeling very blissful after meditating, I heard beautiful, whispering voices, telling me to prepare to meet God. I took this to mean that I was going to die. The idea did not seem at all frightening, so I simply lay down on my bed and waited.

As I lay there, a vast light appeared, moving towards me, and began filling my head. Somehow I sensed that this was an angel, and I asked: 'Are you Gabriel?' There was no reply, but the light became brighter and brighter and began to fill every part of my body with a warm, pulsing energy, like a surge of electricity. The warmth increased to an intense heat, until it was like a fire – but quite painless and not at all alarming; in fact it filled me with energy. I don't know how long this visitation lasted – it may have been seconds or minutes – but during the process I could not move. Eventually the light surged upwards and left through the top of my head.

When I was finally able to sit up, my rational mind clicked into action and I thought, *what* was that? Either that was an archangel or I'd just had some kind of fit! Despite my rational mind, which inevitably questioned what had happened, I continued in a blissful state of consciousness for many days afterwards. During this time I was aware of a constant and clear inner guidance, which helped me understand deep spiritual truths about life; it was as if I had been flooded with knowledge, which came at first as awareness, and only later as words. There was a dramatic change in my perception: I felt able to see into the heart of things, and I experienced a sense of oneness with whatever I looked at – a tree, a flower, an animal – as if I was in direct contact with its essence.

I had a wonderful sense of certainty that everything in the world is just as it is supposed to be. I understood that nothing happens, even to the smallest detail, which is not part of the divine intent, that each event plays a perfect part in the unfolding story of creation. Moreover, we are part of the creative power, so our own intentions play a part in shaping what unfolds. My own life until then had been difficult, but in that state of grace I could see that everything I had gone through had been working towards that moment of revelation. All my spiritual searching had brought me to a point at which I was presented with a gift – even if I did not exactly understand what that gift was.

I continued to hear the beautiful whispering voices that had first spoken to me; they warned me not to say too much about my unusual experiences. I told my parents a little of what had happened; living as I was in an altered state of consciousness, I must have come across to them as quite strange, but fortunately they were very patient with me. At the same time, odd things would happen; for example, people around me would find that their watches had stopped. And I discovered I could influence the results of raffles at the local bazaar – though I was told by my inner guides that I should only do this for the benefit of others.

My rational mind was still trying to understand what had happened, and I looked to experts for advice. The first was a Catholic priest, who just told me to see a doctor! But by one of those lucky 'coincidences', I had the chance of talking to a university professor I knew slightly, who was a Sufi. Unlike the priest, the Sufi believed in angels, and our talks helped me to become more grounded and more trusting of the process I was still going through.

My state of bliss lasted for about three months. During this period I moved back to Oxfordshire – at this time all the practical changes in my life seemed to happen with great ease. I continued to get messages from the beautiful voices; one was that I would meet someone and get married very soon. Six months later I met my husband Will, a musician and songwriter; we have had a remarkable partnership for 30 years, helping each other along our spiritual path through some very difficult times, always with joy and faith.

However, I was still looking for a meaning to what had happened to me. I was faced with a challenge: if my experience was valid, then everything my family and school had taught me about life must come into question. I began reading all kinds of medical literature but could find nothing there that tallied. It was only in the writings of the mystics that I read about experiences similar to mine. Since I could find no scientific explanation, I continued reading spiritual literature, and writing poetry about angels.

I think I had been partly hoping that I *would* find a scientific explanation so that I could put away the event in my mental filing drawer labelled 'unusual happenings' and get on with ordinary life. Traditionally, a visitation by an angel usually includes the announcement of some kind of special task. But my angel had left me no clear instructions. I was, in any case, not at all keen to think I might be called to a mission of some kind, which I might not be up to.

With Will I had two more children and we went to live near Glastonbury, which gave me the peace and quiet I needed to meditate and ask about the meaning of my experiences. One day I took my small daughter in her pushchair for my usual walk in the lovely Somerset countryside. On the way back I suddenly felt a presence behind me – I sensed it as an enormous being growing out of the landscape, stretching up into the sky. The presence felt so awesome that I almost ran home, without daring to look behind me.

A few days later, while I was meditating, I had a powerful inner vision: a picture so clear and precise it was as though I was watching a television screen. I saw a vast angel walking in a landscape like the one outside our house. His head was in the sky, surrounded by a blazing halo, and his wings swept the earth. In his left hand he carried an olive branch, in his right hand a blue crystal. He was wearing a shining white gown, and on his feet were brown sandals; beside him ran a little lamb. Thrilled, I immediately tried painting my vision so that I would remember all the details – I still have a clear picture of him in my mind's eye.

Shortly afterwards I came across a book about angels, describing the Tree of Life, which is a central part of the Jewish mystical tradition, the Kabbalah. The Tree of Life depicts the flow of energy from creation through a series of channels and portals. Each portal has an accompanying archangel who acts as a gatekeeper for a certain kind of spiritual power, such as beauty, strength or compassion. Standing at the foot of the Tree of Life, I learned, is an archangel called Sandalphon, whom I was later able to identify as the archangel of my vision. Sandalphon is a herald for the dawning of the Messianic age when we will live on earth in peace and harmony – the olive branch, of course, symbolises peace, and the lamb is a symbol for the Messiah. Clearly, there was a message here for me.

Following this, I felt guided to work with the Tree of Life, and to undertake a series of meditations in which I asked to meet the other archangels. I also met spiritual guides other than angels, who are still with me. One is a beautiful woman called Astarte, who encourages me to develop wisdom and knowledge without losing touch with the feminine. I also had many conversations with a wise old man with a long white beard and twinkling eyes, who introduced himself as Pythagoras. I learned that, as well as his connection with geometry he was a great esoteric teacher, living about 500 years before Jesus, who preached the kinship of all life and the immortality of the soul.

Another of my inner guides is the archangel of my zodiac sign, Saraquael, who led me to an ancient alphabet called *The Writing of the Angels*, and gave me messages relating to each of these sacred letters. I don't usually regard myself as a channel, but I received these particular messages in the form of automatic writing, using a word processor at five o'clock in the morning – it was rather like taking dictation. They became a collection called *The Angels' Script*, which I published privately. Working with these symbols opened up more inner realms for me – once you are prepared to work with the celestial beings, they will make sure you are kept busy!

Over the last 30 years I have grown to trust my inner guidance. I have explored my past lives, listened to voices and written poetry; I have remembered how to heal and have opened my heart and mind to spiritual messages. In 1988 I wrote my first book, *Discovering Angels*, about my experiences with the archangels on the Tree of Life. I could not get a publisher interested so Will and I set up a company to publish it ourselves. I then began to give talks and run workshops, encouraging others to make similar journeys. Given the lack of interest from publishers, I was surprised by the number of people who not only wanted to hear about angels, but also had already encountered angels themselves.

In fact it is our natural heritage to communicate with and receive help from these intelligent and wise beings who are willing to work with humans to create a better world. If I have a 'mission', it is to keep reminding people that the divine power is within us all and that we can all have access to the timeless wisdom which resides in our hearts.

About This Book

Living with Angels is a guide to the angelic realms, past and present. It is also a guide to a spiritual journey in which you will learn how to communicate and work with angels. I will first introduce you to the angels and other celestial beings who are often classified as angels – including the seraphim, cherubim, archangels and nature spirits. I shall be drawing on ancient and modern accounts of angels making contact with humans, which can be very useful in giving us insights and understanding when we ourselves have angelic experiences. Some angels are awesome, some gentle, some demanding and some encouraging. All are servants of the divine process of creation.

I will then be showing you how to how to communicate with angels, archangels and other spiritual beings, including your guardian angel. Angels are always present all around us, but since they are beings of pure energy we are rarely on the right wavelength to be aware of them, so some inner preparation is needed first. Once you have learned to be in touch with angels, you will find that they will help you on your spiritual path, enabling you to live more intuitively, while feeling safe and supported.

Perhaps you are already on a spiritual path; perhaps you are quite new to all this. In either case, it is my hope that this book will open new doors for you. When we collaborate with the invisible worlds, we move towards a remarkable transformation not only of ourselves but also of humanity as a whole. For it is the task of angels to help to bring the divine plan into reality; by working with them to bring joy and abundance into our own lives we can also help to transform the world around us.

1

Who Are the Angels?

What is an Angel?

The traditional image of an angel is of a beautiful, youthful being with long hair, long robes, a halo and huge wings – although in people's experience today one may just turn up looking like a motor mechanic or a hospital nurse. In fact, although they can take on human or other forms in order to appear visible to our eyes, these celestial beings have no physical attributes: they are vibrational energy fields, endowed with intelligence. If we are sensitive enough to tune into them, or can experience them in meditation, we may see them as glimpses of light and colour, and sometimes hear the music they create. So who, or what energy, created these beings?

Creation Stories

According to traditional accounts of creation, God created angels to be His helpers and messengers. In other words, they are part of the original creation, which is in many ways still a mystery that modern science has yet to solve completely. But religious traditions and scientists both agree that once there was nothing, and then something extraordinary happened and creation began to unfold.

The scientific version tells us that there was a Big Bang that released huge amounts of energy, unleashing a chain of events, which led to the evolution of the universe we live in. According to the world's religions, the driving force behind this process of creation was an awe-inspiring intelligence, which has been given many names, including Allah, Brahma, God and the Great Spirit. When I give workshops, I often ask the group what term they want to use; these days many of us prefer to think in terms of a divine intelligence or divine energy, with whom we can cooperate, rather than the biblical God, who tends to be seen as a white-bearded judge sitting far away in the clouds. Whatever name we give to the Creator, all the religions and creation myths are based on an ultimate truth, interpreted to suit their times and cultures.

The Bible story tells us that God had the idea of creating the great cosmos of which our own solar system is a tiny part, and that when He said, 'Let there be light,' everything started to come into being. In the process, God made a multitude of angels to help Him develop and protect His creation. They are His messengers and servants; God is the creative director, and they act as His personal assistants. In other religious traditions the Creator also has heavenly assistants, called by various names, such as the Immortals of ancient Greece and Rome, and the numerous Hindu gods and goddesses. But unlike some of these gods, angels have no personal desires. They have intelligence, and they have particular roles and functions, but they are there purely to serve creation.

A Bridge between the Worlds

Angels are present in every activity on this planet, and throughout the universe. They act as channels for the energy used by divine intelligence, the energy that we often call the life force, the invisible power that exists in every atom of creation, in every cell in our bodies. The world is alive with this energy – even apparently lifeless objects contain it, such as the table and chairs in your room and the bricks your house is built of. The Indians call this energy *prana*; the Chinese call it *chi*; South Sea Islanders call it *mana*; Christians call it The Holy Spirit. In Hebrew there is a word, *shefa*, the 'everflow', meaning the ever-flowing energy or spirit of the Divine, moving constantly through all creation. It is the angels' task to give it structure and shape, without which it would be formless and undirected. If we compare divine energy to molten gold, it is the task of the angels to set it in an infinite number of moulds, producing an infinite number of creations, from mountains to oceans, from dolphins to birds, from plants to human beings.

Another useful way to think about the role of angels is to imagine that they act as a bridge between the creative ideas of divine intelligence and the end product of those ideas: the material world of the five senses. We tend to think that the spiritual and physical worlds are two separate places, but this is not the case. There are many invisible worlds, interwoven with our own reality and connected to each other by celestial beings. They are go-betweens, coming and going between the invisible worlds of divine intelligence and our own world. They can carry messages in both directions, from the Divine to us, and from us to the world of the Divine. When our messages are prayers or requests – as they so often are – it is not the angels' role to interpret our wants or to interfere with our free will, so we have to take responsibility for the results of our prayers and desires. When you come to work with angels, one of the most important things is to be really clear about your purpose, and to be certain that it is in harmony with the greater good.

The Celestial Hierarchies

We tend to use the word 'angel' in an all-encompassing way to describe celestial beings. In fact, there are many levels of these beings, only some of which are actually angels – archangels, for instance, are not the same as angels. Ever since humans started recording their experiences with angels, scholars have tried to classify them. Seraphim, cherubim, archangels and angels are well known in Judaism, Christianity and Islam, and there are long lists of job descriptions for the various kinds of celestial being. The most famous list of these beings, drawn up around 1,500 years ago, is called The

Celestial Hierarchies. This list describes nine orders of sacred energy, divided into three choirs, each inhabited by three kinds of being:

FIRST CHOIR
  Seraphim
  Cherubim
  Thrones
SECOND CHOIR
  Dominions
  Virtues
  Powers
THIRD CHOIR
  Principalities
  Archangels
  Angels

This list is still referred to today, but in this book we will not be concerned with dominions, principalities and thrones. Ideas about the celestial hierarchies were formulated at a time when earthly princes had great power and ruled over dominions, and the scholars of the time believed that heaven was structured like the society they lived in. I have never come across anyone claiming to have met a dominion or a principality (though I always welcome surprises) and my intuition tells me that these beings were invented to fit in with medieval thinking. We do, however, have reports throughout the ages of meetings with seraphim, cherubim, archangels and angels; the last two are the most usual helpers for human beings.

Changing Helpers

No matter where our helper appears in the hierarchies he or she will be sufficient for our needs.

Moira, a healer acquaintance, has had help from a series of angels over the years; she says they often change when she herself has gone through a shift in her development. When the latest one announced that he was an archangel, Moira thought she must be doing very well. Then she went to a lecture on angels given in a cathedral, at which the speaker described the hierarchy given above. Disappointed to see that archangels come rather low on the list, Moira thought, 'Oh, mine's only a corporal after all!' Whereupon she heard a voice in her head remark, 'But I'm quite good enough for you!'

The Four Worlds

The early Christian scholars spent a great deal of time working out the structure of the invisible worlds. To represent how God brought about creation they drew diagrams showing a series of concentric circles, with God at the centre, causing a series of ripples to flow out from His creative will. When working with the angelic dimensions, I find that this idea can be very useful. Divine energy unfolds from the central source, creating a series of energy fields that vibrate at different frequencies. Like ripples on water, the vibrations slow down as they move out from the source; as they slow down, the pure white light of God breaks down into many colours, the pure sound of God becomes a symphony, and pure energy becomes solid matter.

Different kinds of celestial being emerge at various stages during the process, those closest to the source vibrating at the highest frequency. Humans, who are closest to the earth, and who are materially solid, vibrate at quite a slow rate. Therefore the faster the vibrations of the celestial beings, the harder it is for ordinary human beings to see or hear them.

A good way of working with the invisible dimensions is provided by the Jewish mystical tradition of the Kabbalah. The Kabbalah divides the layers of the creative process into four worlds, as shown in the diagram on the next page. Each world is connected to one of the four elements – fire, air, water and earth – and each world is inhabited by a specific kind of celestial being.

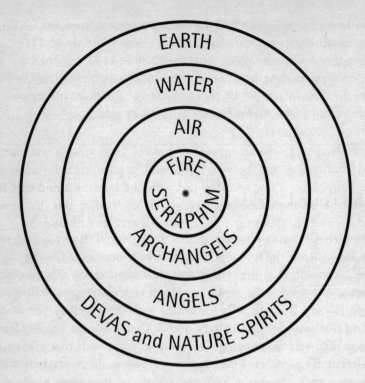

The four worlds

The first world: the seraphim

The seraphim exist in the first world, closest to the source of creation, and therefore vibrating at the highest possible speed. This world is where God conceives His creative desires: it is the place of spiritual love, and it is difficult for us to experience it without an act of complete self-surrender. The seraphim are totally bound up in the divine love and are said to spend their time singing continuously: '*Kadoish, Kadoish, Kadoish*' ('Holy, Holy, Holy'). They are pictured as faces surrounded by wings, looking rather like flowers; I think of them as petals on a rose, whose centre is God.

The word 'seraph' comes from the Hebrew word *sarap* (to burn).

The love of God is like fire, an all-consuming passion for creating life. Fire, then, is the element of this first world. Human encounters with seraphim are rare, but not unheard of. In an anthology of religious experiences* a modern Christian describes how he was praying out loud in his room, thanking God for changing his life, when, quite suddenly, he was overtaken by a 'swirling force of burning joy'. He felt that the force might shatter his body as if it were an eggshell, yet at the same time it was warm and comforting, and he was filled with 'a pure consciousness of the Truth'. After a few seconds, just when he became afraid that he would be 'extinguished', the energy left him. After this, he never had any doubts about the power and personal love of God.

This experience is very similar to my own first angelic encounter. I have since come to believe that I was visited by a seraph, because the light that went through my body felt like fire – a painless and energising fire – which left me with no verbal message, but filled me with a feeling of certainty and joy.

An encounter with the seraphim is usually unexpected, and clearly a very powerful experience, which seems to demand considerable personal development beforehand. I would not advise people to seek contact with them without a good deal of preparation and personal guidance.

The second world: the archangels

The archangels exist in the second world where the vibrations are beginning to slow down, but are still too fast for us to perceive with

---

* *Seeing the Invisible: Modern religious and transcendent experiences*, Meg Maxwell and Verna Tschudin, eds, Oxford: RERC, 1990.

Sir Alister Hardy was an Oxford professor of marine biology who had a life-long interest in the spiritual nature of man. In 1968 he set up a research unit in Oxford to study spiritual experiences. In 1969, in response to a national appeal, the unit was flooded with several thousand letters from ordinary people of all religions and none who had had encounters with angels or experienced a sense of the Divine in other ways. These are now in an archive in the University of Wales.

our ordinary senses; the energy is subtle and intangible, like air, which is their element. This world is where the divine intelligence makes decisions and begins to organise creation at a fundamental level, and the archangels assist with this planning. They are like architects: they carry the blueprints for creation and our ongoing evolution.

The most famous archangels are Michael, Gabriel and Raphael: the only three recognised by the Catholic Church. Most people working with angelic traditions know that a fourth archangel, Auriel or Uriel, works with the famous three, in order to complete a set of governors who preside over the four directions and the four elements.

Michael is the commander in chief of all the archangels and brings courage and leadership to those who work with him; he governs the south and the element of fire. His colour is golden yellow.

Gabriel governs the west and the element of air – though some traditions associate him with water. He is the messenger, bringing inspiration and the spiritual gifts of insight and communication, so I believe he is most at home in the air element. His colours are turquoise and bright yellow.

Raphael governs the east and the element of water; he is the divine physician and brings compassion, empathy and healing. Some traditions associate Raphael with the air element, but the nurturing quality brought by this archangel seems to me to be more in keeping with the water element. His colours are rose and lilac, which are the colours of crystals, such as amethyst and rose quartz, often used by healers.

Auriel (sometimes spelt Uriel) governs the north and the element of earth. Auriel is at once tender and strong, bringing a protective, solid and enduring quality. There is a mothering aspect to Auriel's care and his colours are silver and pale blue. Although the Roman Catholic Church does not recognise Auriel, he has a feast day (28 July) in the Egyptian and Ethiopian Church calendars.

As well as these four, there are many, many more archangels, some of whom we will be meeting later on in Chapters 9 and 10. Most of our knowledge about them comes through the Jewish tradition, which is a great deal older than Christianity.

The archangels can often seem quite awe-inspiring and rather distant from everyday human needs. Because they are concerned with the bigger picture, it is not really their task to help us with daily problems. Each archangel has a specific area of activity, and does not step outside this area. For example, there are archangels who oversee rites of passage, such as childbirth, marriage and death – but don't expect Michael to find you a parking space! When angels appear to humans, it is usually to announce revelations of the divine plan, or to support groups of people, rather than to help individuals.

Grethe's Story

Sometimes angels allow people simply to be aware of their presence – as in the case of Grethe, a healer whom I met in Norway.

Often people who come to my workshops ask me how to identify whether they have experienced an angel or an archangel. Grethe, who was on a course I was teaching in Bergen, took me aside to tell me about her experience. One day she was knitting by her window overlooking the sea when she heard an extraordinary sound of singing; looking out, she saw a vast angelic being, stretching its luminous wings across the wide vista of the ocean, from one edge of the horizon to the other. As she described this, Grethe's face was alight, and I could sense the radiance pouring from her, so much so that I could feel what she felt at the time.

I thought that the being she had seen must have been an archangel because of its sheer size, and also because it said nothing personal to her. She had evidently been given a glimpse of the great power of a seascape archangel; perhaps his task is to watch over the fishermen of that part of the Norwegian coast.

By the way, it is very important to come to an understanding of your own experiences based on your own instincts and intuition rather than on information from someone else. For example, someone might say to me, 'I always experience Michael surrounded by blue, but you say his colour is yellow.' My answer is to trust your own experience. Colour especially is very much an individual matter.

Archangels may ask individuals to take on tasks that will be for the greater benefit of humanity. If this should happen to you, you will find your personal life is disrupted and you will have to make big adjustments – in fact, your whole life may seem to fall apart. Classic examples are the Archangel Gabriel announcing to the Virgin Mary that she is to give birth to Jesus, and the same archangel visiting the Prophet Mohammed to give him the Koran – both hugely life-changing events!

On the other hand, you can seek and receive guidance from archangels, particularly the archangel of your sign of the zodiac (see Chapter 9). You naturally come under the wings of many archangels. There is an archangel for your nation and one for any spiritual group or religion that you may belong to.

The third world: angels and guardian angels

The angels exist in the third world, and for humans they are the most familiar of the celestial beings. The element associated with this third world is water, which relates to the loving, almost maternal emotional support the angels give us.

Nowadays many people are experiencing angels in their everyday lives, especially at times of crisis, but also in moments of tranquillity and beauty. There are many reports of angels appearing as human beings in order to help someone in a dangerous situation. These 'people' appear at just the right moment, then immediately disappear, leaving no trace. Afterwards, those who have been rescued often remember something curious – it may have been raining yet the helper's clothes were dry, or perhaps their clothes looked rather old-fashioned.

The angels can cross into our world in the twinkling of an eye, and we can easily meet them if we open our hearts and minds. The divine intelligence has created the angelic world to be like a mother to us, nurturing and protecting us like a baby in the womb; angels are always available to heal and soothe. Guardian angels belong to this group: they have an ongoing task to nurture each individual, guiding us and chiding when necessary. If an angel steps in to prevent you being run over as you cross a busy road, this may well be your guardian angel.

Our Guardian Angels

Here are two good examples of the kind of intervention we may expect from a guardian angel, who is watching out for us wherever we go.

Jenny, one of my home-study students, told me of an incident that happened when she went to work a few months after her son was born. She was crossing the forecourt at London Bridge station, not realising that buses used the area, when she was suddenly aware of a warm pressure on her forehead, which brought her to a halt – just as a fast-moving bus shot in front of her. Jenny says that the driver had definitely not seen her and she would certainly have been killed if she had taken another step.

Another of my students, Daphne, told me a similar story. One evening, while walking to her bus-stop after work, she had started to cross the road at a busy 'green man' crossing when a car came straight at her. The people inside were talking to each other; they had not seen the traffic lights or Daphne, and weren't going to stop. Daphne went on: 'At the same time as I was taking this in, there was a shaft of heat, like a sheath, which shot around me in an instant and it was as if I wasn't in the road. The car didn't hit me; the people in it didn't see me. I turned around and shouted at the car and then I realised that time had stood still because, despite all the people around me, no one looked at me when I shouted; no one said, "That was close!" Then everything returned to normal – noise, people, traffic and me walking up to the bus-stop, knowing that an angel had moved me out of the way, because it "wasn't time yet".'

Your guardian has been with you from before your birth. My own experience is that mine has been with me throughout many lifetimes.

He is not just helping me during this incarnation, but assisting me throughout the journey of my soul, until my soul's purpose is completed. I will be saying more about how you can maintain a powerful contact with your guardian in Chapter 5.

Here I should say a little about the soul. My own understanding is that the soul is the part of us that is eternal: it is an ever-growing, ever-evolving energy field that is a spark of the divine intelligence manifested in the physical body. This spark comes into incarnation, sometimes on earth, sometimes elsewhere, in order to explore different possibilities and gain knowledge and experience, and always seeking to find higher forms of expression. Its purpose is to evolve over many lifetimes to higher and higher levels of being, until it can return to the Divine Source.

THE HIGHER SELF, GUARDIAN ANGELS, AND SPIRIT GUIDES

People often ask me what the difference is between the guardian angel and the higher self, and whether spirit guides are the same as guardian angels.

The higher self is the highest part of our consciousness; it is the point of contact between the soul and the human personality we have chosen for this lifetime. It is the best part of our human self; the part that is open to spiritual messages and that understands our deep connection not only to all humanity but also to all creation. It is the higher self that is able to hear messages from the guardian angel. When we are busily going about our everyday lives, we do not always use this faculty, which is why it is so important to allow time for regular meditation and to create opportunities for retreat from everyday bustle. When we meditate we allow the higher self to open up, like a flower, and we are able to connect to many other beings – including our guardian angel and perhaps other helpers in the invisible world.

Our guardian angel is our personal guide and teacher – our mentor, who has been with us since before we were born. The Greek philosopher Plato describes how each soul chooses its journey and then connects with the guardian angel before being born. If you are interested in past lives, you may discover, as I did, that the same guardian angel has been accompanying you through many incarnations – even if they have not all been human ones, or even on this planet.

We can also receive guidance from the spirits of people who have lived and died, who have been connected to us through friendship or family ties. While your guardian angel is the most important of your helpers, a deceased parent, grandparent or child may provide wise guidance too. These spirit guides may even come from the animal kingdom. Angels have never incarnated as human beings. They can take on the appearance of being human, but they do not incarnate.

At some stage our spirit helpers may evolve and move on to another incarnation, but as long as we need them they will not fail to help us, wherever they are. And their loving support for us helps them to evolve too. While our guardian angel remains constant, spirit guides may alter over time or according to our needs.

We can also call on the guidance of other higher beings, such as ascended masters – spirits who have lived a highly spiritual life on earth and have taken on the task of helping us from a higher plane (Pythagoras is one of these). If you lived in a spiritual community in a past life you would have easy access to a master, male or female, who was your teacher in that life. Even if you have no memories of this kind of past life, and feel you are starting from scratch, you are entitled to ask for help from any of these advanced souls. We can all have access to the wisdom that they have developed over the centuries. Some people receive guidance from intelligent beings from other planets or galaxies.

There is plenty of help available on many levels and our higher self is able to assist the soul in its evolution by reaching out for this help. We only have to ask.

The fourth world: devas, nature spirits and elementals

Devas, nature spirits, fairies and elementals are not classed as angels and live in the fourth world as we humans do. This fourth world, represented by the element of earth, is the world where material things come into being. Alongside humans are many invisible spirits who help with the nuts and bolts of nature. And we can ask for and obtain their help in the natural world – in our gardens, for instance.

Although these spirits whiz around so fast we rarely see them, they still have slower vibrations than angels. They are tied to the natural cycles of our planet, just as we are. The task of the nature spirits, devas and elementals is to protect the natural world, while we humans are stewards whose duty it is to cooperate with all four worlds.

Fairies and nature spirits are not just characters in legends and children's stories; they do exist, and humans can have contact with them. Even today, many people, especially those working in the countryside or in gardens, do see these magical helpers. The founders of the Findhorn community in Scotland were helped and advised by the devas – higher nature spirits – who were directly involved in creating an amazing garden in sandy soil. My father-in-law, who is a very practical man not given to fancy, and my even more down-to-earth mother-in-law, both told me they had seen fairies. They lived in an industrial area where you might not expect to see nature spirits.

Nature spirits are usually attached to a single place or object, such as a tree, or a rock or lake. In the Middle Ages they were often described by country folk as mischief-makers. Shakespeare's character Puck, for instance, is the spirit of the wood, and creates havoc for the human lovers who get lost there on Midsummer's Eve. Woods still have their spirits. Quite recently I heard of a very sceptical young man who camped out in a wood one night and suddenly woke to find a green lady lying on the branch of a tree, staring at him. Thinking he was dreaming, he closed his eyes and opened them again. She was still there.

The term 'elemental' embraces all kinds of spirit being who help to create and maintain the natural world – elves, brownies, fairies and goblins are all elementals. But there are four particular kinds of elemental who work with the four elements: gnomes for the earth element, sylphs for air, undines for water and salamanders for fire. Their task is to ensure harmony in the natural world, even if this means creating events that humans don't like, such as storms and earthquakes.

Nature spirits and elementals are all answerable to angels. Like humans living on this planet, they exist in the world of time. They do not have ongoing souls, nor can they move into the timeless world, as the angels can, and as we do when we leave our present incarnations. If our own world ceased to exist, the nature spirits and elementals would no longer have a job to do and they would also cease to exist. But the angels, archangels and seraphim would continue, as long as divine intelligence was busy creating other worlds. And our souls would continue journeying towards their spiritual goal.

The fifth element: the cherubim

There is one group of celestial beings I have not described so far: the cherubim. I have left them until last because, while all the others belong to just one of the four worlds, the cherubim live in all four, and the element they work with interpenetrates all four (see the diagram on the next page). This mysterious fifth element, or *quinta essentia*, has sometimes been described as 'ether' – an invisible, magical substance which cannot be identified by the senses. Today we can understand it as *prana* or *chi*, the energy that flows through the activities of the four elements, providing continuity throughout the system.

The cherubim are the most awesome and powerful spiritual beings ever described. The Hebrew word *kerub*, from which 'cherub' derives, means 'fullness of knowledge'. Although they are second in rank to the seraphim, the cherubim oversee and move through all the four worlds. They encourage the flow of holiness throughout creation, so that universal truths will never be lost.

These awe-inspiring beings should not be confused with the kinds of cherub who appear in pictures as chubby babies with dimpled bottoms. In the Bible the cherubim are described as having four wings and four faces: a lion, a man, an eagle and a bull. These correspond with the zodiac signs of Leo, Aquarius, Scorpio and Taurus, which in turn each relate to the four elements: fire, air, water and earth. So the cherubim are able to see from all four directions, and watch over all the levels of creation. The Bible tells us that the

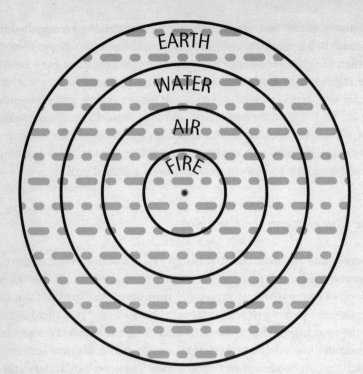

The realm of the cherubim

entrance to the Garden of Eden was constantly guarded by cherubim with flaming swords.

Encounters with cherubim are very rare (though a vivid description is given in the Bible by the prophet Ezekiel). But when we come to work with angels, it can be useful to be aware of the existence of these all-powerful, omnipresent beings and their relationship with the energy that underlies all creation.

Working with the Angels

These, then, are the angels and other spiritual beings with whom we can all learn to work in order to enhance our lives and help us on our spiritual journey. Just how we can do this is explained from Chapter 4 onwards. Meanwhile, l would like to introduce you to some more of the celestial beings who have affected the lives of human beings from the earliest days of history.

2

Angels Through History

Angels in Antiquity

If you go to the British Museum in London you can see some of the earliest – and most powerful – images of winged figures: majestic sculptures and carvings from the Assyrian and Babylonian kingdoms, which date back to around 900 BC. It is exciting and rather extraordinary to be able to get off a London bus and enter the visionary world of people who lived nearly 3,000 years ago. (Similar sculptures can be found in the Louvre in Paris and the Metropolitan Museum in New York.)

One huge statue, which acted as gatekeeper to a royal palace, has a human face with a curling beard and hair, the body of a bull and huge, angelic wings. Other supernatural figures are shown in relief carvings; some have human heads, some the heads of eagles, and all have wings – sometimes two, sometimes four. Many of these are Assyrian angels shown using a pinecone to sprinkle holy water over a sacred tree and the people around them.

If ever you get a chance to see these beautiful sculptures you will really get in touch with the awesome power that ancient people experienced when they met angels; because these amazing beings, traditionally referred to as 'genies', can be regarded as angels: they were protective spirits, guarding not only palaces but also individuals from evil influences. It is possible that the mystics and priests of the time saw them in visions and then instructed craftsmen to create sculptures from their descriptions.

Angels have visited humans throughout recorded history; they appear in the very earliest books of the Bible and are an essential part of Jewish, Christian and Islamic traditions. Protective spirits also appear in other cultures, under different names. The angels we are meeting in this chapter are known to us because mystics and prophets have met them, scholars have debated about them, poets have written about them and artists have painted them.

The word angel comes from the Greek word *angelos*, meaning 'messenger'. In Sanskrit there is a similar word, *angiras*, meaning 'divine spirit'. The Hebrew word for angel is *malakh*, which also means 'king' or 'royal one'. Some archangels, such as Michael, are referred to in the Bible as 'princes', based on the idea that God held a 'court' in heaven; this was reflected on earth by worldly kings who were given their earthly power by God. In today's more democratic world, we can think of the 'kingdom' as the spiritual part of ourselves.

The stories that have come down to us, particularly in the Bible, tell us how our ancestors communicated with powerful celestial beings; their descriptions of seraphim and cherubim and visitations from archangels help us to understand our relationship with the Divine. And, importantly, they explain how our ancestors received knowledge and wisdom from these powerful beings.

Take astrology, for example, which originated in ancient Babylon. Angels have strong associations with the stars, and I feel certain that the knowledge of astrology was channelled to the Babylonian priests by the angels. When the priests studied the skies they would have entered a meditative state, enabling them to receive the information. Much human knowledge has come to us in this way, and still does; it may take the form of major artistic inspiration, or small but helpful insights; for example, even if we don't see angels, it is quite common for us to feel prompted to do something which turns out to be just the right thing at exactly the right time. Or we need a piece of information, and a book falls open at exactly the right page. The angels are always at work.

Angels in the Bible

The Hebrew Bible (the Old Testament) recounts the many trials, tribulations, wars and exiles inflicted on the Israelites – the ancient

Jewish people. At regular intervals in their history, particularly in times of crisis, prophets would appear – spiritual teachers who channelled messages from God to teach, encourage or chastise the Israelites. Many of these prophets were visited by 'the angel of the Lord', who turns up in several biblical events. Whether in fact these stories refer to one angel or more we can't tell; it was not until after the Israelites had been in captivity in Babylon that angels were given names.

In one very famous story, the 'angel of the Lord' appeared to Moses 'in a flame of fire' in the middle of a bush which seemed to be on fire without burning up. From the centre of this burning bush, God then spoke to Moses. In another well-known story, God told Abraham that he must prove his love for Him by sacrificing his son Isaac; at the last minute the angel of the Lord appeared and stopped him, announcing that God had been 'just testing'.

During the Israelite wars with the Assyrians, the Assyrian army was sent to attack Jerusalem, and 'it came to pass that night, that the angel of the Lord went out and smote in the camp of the Assyrians a hundred fourscore and five thousand: and ... early in the morning, behold they were all dead corpses'. Whoever this angel or archangel was, he seems to have been a force to be reckoned with. We also hear of him destroying cities whenever God felt that the Israelites weren't living up to His very high standards. In fact, since angels are not usually destructive or aggressive, it is likely that these incidents were the results of natural causes, or courageous fighting by the Israelites, strengthened by the conviction that the Lord and his angels were fighting for their side. Powerful beliefs are in themselves energetic forces.

The biblical prophets had more creative experiences with some magnificent and awe-inspiring celestial beings – not the gentle angels we think of as our helpers nowadays. Perhaps these holy men were able to experience the more fiery aspects of the Divine because they lived simple lives in the desert and their minds were less cluttered with the kinds of distraction we experience in modern life. (And most of us would not be very happy if these grand characters were to interrupt our everyday routines!)

The prophet Isaiah, for example, was called to his mission by a wonderful vision of the seraphim. One day, when he was in the temple, he had a vision of God seated on a high throne. God's robe filled the temple and He was surrounded by seraphim, each with six wings – two to cover its face, two to cover its feet and two to fly with. And the seraphim were singing a never-ending song: 'Holy, Holy, Holy, Lord God of Hosts, the whole earth is full of His Glory'. As they chanted, the foundations of the temple began to shake and Isaiah was very afraid, believing he was not good enough to see God. But one of the seraphim brought a hot coal from the altar and touched Isaiah's mouth with it, saying: 'Behold, this has touched your lips; your guilt is taken away, and your sin is forgiven.'

The seraphim's song of 'Holy, Holy, Holy!' (*Kadoish, Kadoish, Kadoish* in Hebrew, and *Sanctus, Sanctus, Sanctus* in Latin) is included in both Christian and Jewish religious services, and many great composers have set these words to music. For thousands of years, many generations of religious people have been repeating Isaiah's visionary poetry in order to connect themselves to the power of the Divine.

About a hundred years after Isaiah, when the Israelites were in captivity in Babylon, the prophet Ezekiel had a number of visions, which he describes in the book of Ezekiel in the Old Testament. In the first, he met four cherubim who arrived in a whirlwind in a bright cloud, flashing with amber-coloured fire. They resembled humans, but each had four faces: the face of a man, the face of a lion, the face of a bull and the face of an eagle. Each had four wings; they were as bright as burning coals or fiery torches, and they moved like flashes of lightning. Above them appeared a being resembling a man, seated on a sapphire throne, glowing with light and surrounded by a rainbow, who gave Ezekiel God's message for the Israelites.

Gabriel the Messenger

The amazing beings who appeared to Isaiah and Ezekiel did not have individual names. You may be surprised to learn that the first archangel to be named in the Bible is Satan, who appears in the book of Job as God's tester. He is a very interesting character, who may not be as wicked as is generally believed; I shall be talking more about him in Chapter 7.

The next celestial visitors to be named are Gabriel and Michael, both of whom appear in the book of Daniel. Daniel was one of the Israelites who were exiled to the kingdom of Babylon; he became the interpreter of dreams for the Babylonian King, Nebuchadnezzar. Gabriel appeared to Daniel in human form, and helped Daniel interpret his own visions. In the same book, Michael is described as a prince, and as God's chief helper, with a special commission to watch over the nation of Israel.

For Christians, Gabriel's most famous message must be the one he brought to Mary, announcing the conception of Jesus. There are many beautiful paintings of the Annunciation, in which Gabriel is shown presenting Mary with a lily, a symbol of purity, while he tells her that her baby is a gift of the Holy Spirit. Although his name is not mentioned, many Christians believe that it was also Gabriel who announced Christ's birth to the shepherds and advised Mary and Joseph to escape to Egypt when Herod's soldiers were hunting the newborn King. It is also believed that Gabriel rolled away the stone that had sealed Jesus' tomb, after the Resurrection.

Gabriel plays a major role in the Islamic religion, too, since he delivered the Koran to the Prophet Muhammed. The story goes that Muhammed underwent a purification carried out by angels: they visited him in his sleep, opened his chest, washed his heart clean of doubt and false beliefs, and then filled it with wisdom poured from a golden vessel, before sewing him up again. Gabriel then took the Prophet on a magical night journey, riding on the back of a supernatural horse, called the Buraq, and visiting the seven heavens. The Prophet describes Gabriel as having 600 wings set with red crystals; he is whiter and brighter than the snow, with a diadem of light on his brow, inscribed: 'There is no God but God'.

In all these stories, Gabriel acts as God's chief messenger; he announces special events, bringing spiritual knowledge and understanding. He is rather like Mercury, the messenger god of the

Romans (known as Hermes in Greek mythology), who was also famous as a guardian of wisdom.

Angels in the Middle Ages and the Renaissance

The artists of Islam – like the Jews – were forbidden to depict images of living things; their artistic talents were devoted to beautiful calligraphy and abstract designs. But there was no such prohibition in Christianity, and Christian artists have illustrated biblical stories and characters from the very beginning. In the Middle Ages churches and cathedrals throughout Europe were full of colour, beautifully decorated with wall paintings, carvings and statues of saints and angels, especially of the great archangels Gabriel, Michael and Raphael.

Most of the great art at that time was to be found in churches because the popes and bishops were extremely wealthy and could afford to patronise the arts. Many old churches in Europe still display wall paintings depicting biblical tales of human encounters with angels. Before printing was invented in the 15th century, ordinary people had no books and few were able to read, so their knowledge of Bible stories and of angels came largely from these story paintings. Christians took their religion very seriously in those times, and the painters, often monks, who created these images, were inspired by genuine faith and belief. Very possibly their paintings were based on visions seen during prayer and meditation.

Many of the beautiful angel pictures you will come across today on Christmas cards and in angel books were painted during the Renaissance in the 15th and 16th centuries; they can still be seen in the galleries and churches of Italian cities like Florence and Venice. They show angels as we traditionally know them, with wings, long robes and halos; many are shown singing and playing musical instruments on the walls and ceilings of cathedrals and churches.

St Joan of Arc

People's belief during the Middle Ages was so strong that when a pious French country girl heard celestial voices announcing that God had a mission for her, she was able to persuade the most powerful people in the land of the truth of her visions.

St Joan of Arc (1412–31) was only 13 when she first heard a voice, accompanied by a blaze of light, which she identified as the Archangel Michael accompanied by other angels; they were joined by St Margaret and St Catherine. As time went on they instructed her that she must lead the French army against the English, with whom France was at war. This young, uneducated girl succeeded in convincing the authorities of the court and the army, as well as a committee of churchmen, and actually led the French soldiers into battle. Regrettably, politics later entered the picture. When she was captured, the priests and judges – who were on the side of the English – ignored the previous judgement of the church committee and declared that her voices were diabolical. In the end, at not yet 20, she was burned as a witch, still declaring loyalty to her voices.

Dr Dee and the Language of the Angels

During the Middle Ages and the Renaissance, anyone experiencing visions or seeking spiritual knowledge was in danger of being accused of witchcraft, but this didn't stop the curious from their investigations. The great minds of the day – like modern scientists – were intrigued by the mysteries of the universe. The scholars of those times were also astrologers, and many were fascinated by alchemy, a sort of magical chemistry whose aim was to turn base metals like lead into gold. Some of them even claimed to have achieved this.

One of the most famous of these alchemists was Dr John Dee (1527–1608), a highly regarded scholar who was court astrologer to

Queen Elizabeth I of England. It was Dr Dee who decided which day would be the most auspicious for her coronation – he seems to have chosen well, because she had a long and glorious reign. Dr Dee was a brilliant man, highly educated and an expert in mathematics and navigation, whose aim was to uncover the secrets of the material world. Today, he would probably be a quantum physicist, but in Dee's time, probing the secrets of the universe meant delving into the mind of God.

Dr Dee believed that this could be achieved with the help of the angels, who were in direct contact with God. He therefore devoted all his energy to trying to communicate with angels in order to acquire the knowledge he wanted – nothing less than the key to the secrets of the entire universe. He decided to do this by means of 'scrying' – gaining psychic information by gazing into crystals and 'magic' mirrors. If you go to the British Museum to see the Assyrian angels, you can also see Dee's crystal and the obsidian mirror that he used. His magical table inscribed with occult symbols is on display in the Ashmolean Museum in Oxford.

Dee did not have clairvoyant gifts and was not successful at scrying, but he acquired the assistance of a gifted medium – a rather dubious character called Edward Kelley. Using the crystal, Kelley was able to contact a large number of angels and spirits, and John Dee set about conducting a series of experiments with him, which he recorded meticulously in his notebooks. These notebooks and Dr Dee's *Spiritual Diaries* are still in existence.

In them Dee recounts how the angels who appeared to Kelley in the crystal dictated over a period of months a totally unknown secret language. They told him that this was the original divine language, used by the angels and by Adam and Eve before they were expelled from Paradise. Translated, the angelic message is very poetic and rather obscure, but at this point in the story, it certainly seems to have come from the angels. It is highly unlikely that Kelley, who was only moderately well educated, could have invented a complete language – and experts agree that it is a genuine language, with its own alphabet, grammar and numerical system.

Although Dr Dee claimed to be on a spiritual quest for sacred truths, his diaries demonstrate that he plagued the angels with all kinds of trivial questions. But his most dangerous activity was his alchemical quest to create the 'philosopher's stone', which would turn ordinary metal into gold. Dee may not have been greedy for personal wealth, but he depended for his income on wealthy patrons, and needed to convince them that he could deliver the goods – and his obsessive need to achieve a material result was to lead to his downfall.

Dee worked Kelley harder and harder, making him scry for hours on end, which affected his health and mental stability. As the experiments moved on, Kelley began to think they were meddling in black magic, rather than uncovering spiritual wisdom. It was a combination of Kelley's fear and Dee's ambition that led them into a very dark episode. They found themselves receiving communications from so-called 'angels' whom Kelley feared were demons.

This may well have been the case, since these beings came up with the instruction that Kelley and Dee should swap wives! This was an unthinkable proposition in those days, totally against all Christian teachings, and guaranteeing an eternity in Hell. As you can imagine, Mrs Dee and Mrs Kelley were hysterical at the suggestion. But Dr Dee was so obsessed by his quest that he would do anything the so-called angels requested – in fact they threatened him that unless they obeyed, God would strike them all dead – and so the wives were given no option and the swap took place. After this episode, there were no more 'angelic conversations' and Kelley and Dee parted company.

In the end, everything went wrong for Dr Dee. He acquired a reputation as a black magician; Shakespeare depicted him as the magician Prospero in *The Tempest*, and the playwright, Christopher Marlowe, used him as the basis for his character of Dr Faustus, who sold his soul to the Devil in exchange for wealth and power. An angry mob ransacked his vast library and destroyed his scientific instruments. Eventually he died a very sad, very poor old man, still defending his claim that he was talking to angels, not demons, and that his desire was only to understand deep cosmic truths.

Angels and Demons

From where we stand we can see that John Dee was kidding himself, and that his ambition had taken such a strong root that he was prepared to override the sanctity of marriage. Dr Dee's early experiences seem to have been with genuine angels, but in his single-minded quest for knowledge he laid himself open to negative energies which played havoc with his family life, resulting in a great deal of sadness and misery.

Dr Dee's story provides us with an important lesson in dealing with the invisible worlds. In the New Age today more and more people are developing powerful healing and psychic gifts; but without strong ethical values and one's feet firmly on the ground it is possible to be carried away by the power and glamour of it all, and forget to question one's motivation. As St Paul wrote: 'Though I speak in the tongues of men and of angels ... and if I have the gift of prophecy and understand all mysteries, and if I have all faith, so that I could remove mountains, but have not love, I am nothing.'

So it is wise to be discriminating about the psychic and spiritual teachers we go to, and to be aware of how we use our own spiritual gifts. We must ask the angels only for help which is appropriate for our needs and in harmony with the needs of others. Anyone who calls on their powers to support greed and ambition is at risk of attracting darker forces. So when you are working with angels, always ask: 'Is my work creating loving possibilities for everyone I know, as well as for myself?'

In Dr Dee's time the Catholic Church constantly questioned mystical experiences: it was vital to be able to distinguish between real angels and demons pretending to be angels. During this period a Spanish mystic, St Teresa of Avila (1515–82) was also experiencing numerous visions and often saw angels. Her most famous vision has often been illustrated in paintings and sculpture as the Ecstasy of St Teresa: this was a visitation from an angel 'who seemed to be all afire' and who pierced her heart with a flaming spear, leaving her 'completely afire with a great love of God'. In her autobiography, Teresa tells how her Catholic confessors tried persistently to convince her that her visions were from the devil. She was tactful with the confessors, but learned how to discern her own reality for herself.

In distinguishing true visions from false, spiritual teachers from different cultures will usually tell you to use your own traditional teachings as a guide; for example, Dr Dee should have known that the spirits he had summoned were mischievous when they told him to go against the teachings of Christianity.

The Reformation: the Angels Are Banished

During the lifetimes of Dr Dee and St Teresa an enormous upheaval was taking place in the religious life of Europe, in the form of the Reformation. This was the Protestant movement aimed at reforming Western Christianity, which ultimately led to the separation of the Protestant and Roman Catholic Churches. Over the centuries the Roman Catholic Church had become increasingly powerful and wealthy, and its leaders more and more corrupt. The movement of protest was launched in 1512 by a German monk called Martin Luther. During the 16th century many changes took place very rapidly, helped along by the new technology of printing and the translation of the Bible into everyday languages.

As the flood of change gathered energy, some ruling princes and kings took the opportunity to claim new power for themselves. The Tudor King Henry VIII broke with the Roman Church and declared himself Head of his own Church of England – partly because the Pope refused to give him a divorce. In 1536 Henry closed down all the monasteries and seized Church wealth for himself. In a wave of anti-Catholicism throughout England and northern Europe churches were raided, statues of saints and angels were destroyed (they were considered 'idolatrous'), stained-glass windows were smashed and the richly painted walls of churches were whitewashed over.

Over the next hundred years the Protestants became more and more strict; even stricter were the group who called themselves Puritans and wore nothing but black. The Protestants wanted everything to be very simple, including churches and chapels. After centuries of highly elaborate ritual this was understandable, and anyone who attends a Quaker meeting, or goes to a Methodist chapel, will appreciate meditating in a quiet, uncluttered space. But quite a few beautiful babies went out with the bath water – including the angels. With everyone now able to read the Bible, the power of the written word replaced the power of the image. In southern Europe the Catholic Church kept a stronghold and there are still wonderful pictures of angels in the churches of Italy, southern France and Spain. But the pioneers who sailed to the Americas were Protestants, and their churches and chapels were also built in the simple style – they were angel-free zones!

Christianity had been in serious need of reform, but the sad part was that the new approach discouraged the use of the imaginative abilities – and the imagination provides an important pathway to spiritual experience, particularly the visual imagination. (I shall be saying more about this in Chapter 5). This is one reason why, in many parts of Christendom, angels went out of fashion. Although they have many powers, the angels cannot override human thought, and if our inner doors are closed it is difficult for them to make their presence felt.

But whenever there is an opening, the angels will ensure that our visionary gifts are kept alive. The freedom from Catholic restrictions did allow a number of Christian mystics to speak publicly about their visions without fear of disapproval. Even though the Protestant churches became very powerful in northern Europe, the angels found a champion in Sweden, in the person of Emanuel Swedenborg, son of a Lutheran bishop. Born in 1688, Swedenborg was a brilliant engineer and scientist, who published books on mineralogy, astronomy and anatomy. When he was 56 his life was changed by a vision of Jesus, which led him to give up his previous work and dedicate himself to mystical research. He communicated with the angels, who gave him detailed descriptions of heaven and Hell which Emanuel then published in his rather heavy-going books.

One of Swedenborg's most important messages was that 'in no sense can we say that heaven is outside us – it is within'. His teachings were often very challenging for his time. For example, he said that anyone could go to heaven, not just Christians, as long as they had lived a life of love and charity. After his death, Swedenborg's followers established various churches and societies. One of these, the Church of the New Jerusalem, was founded in London in 1788. Among the people who joined it were a hard-working but poor illustrator and his wife, Mr and Mrs William Blake.

William Blake Sees Angels in London

The highly imaginative painter and poet William Blake (1757–1827) initially worked mainly as an illustrator of other people's books, but later created wonderful engravings of his own visions and illustrations of his own poems. He lived in London, which was much smaller and dirtier than it is now – there was no traffic pollution, but the drainage system left a great deal to be desired. However, a natural mystic will be open to the hidden worlds of angels, wherever they live. Blake's pictures were often inspired by the visions that he saw from childhood. When he was about eight years old he saw 'a tree filled with angels' on Peckham Rye Common; he wrote later, 'Their bright wings covered the tree boughs like stars.' He continued to have visions all through his life, of Christ and other biblical and mystical figures as well as angels.

By the time William was born, the Reformation had passed its peak, and during the 18th century the philosophical movement known as the Enlightenment was encouraging thinkers to become more scientific and rationalistic in their approach to creation. This new-found freedom of thought meant that some people were even suggesting that God might not exist. William Blake, however, regarded reason as the enemy of imagination, which he valued highly; he also believed that the increasing industrialisation of society was destroying people's innocent connection to heaven and the angels. Discovering the teachings of Swedenborg must have been very significant for him, and strengthened his belief in his own angels.

His diaries record how one day he was musing in his study, having been commissioned to create an angel as an illustration for a book. 'Who can paint an angel?' he asked himself aloud.

Then he heard a voice saying: 'Michelangelo could.' William looked around and could see no one, although he noticed that the room was lighter than usual.

'How do *you* know?' he asked his invisible visitor.

The voice replied: 'I *know*, for I sat for him. I am the Archangel Gabriel.'

William was somewhat suspicious. 'Oh, you are, are you? I must have better assurance than that of a wandering voice; you may be an evil spirit – there are such in the land.'

The voice replied: 'You shall have good assurance. Can an evil spirit do this?'

William became aware of a shining shape, with bright wings, which radiated a great light. As he watched, the shape grew larger and larger. The angel waved his hands and the roof of the study opened as he rose up into heaven. Then, William tells us, Gabriel stood in the sun and 'moved the universe'. Unfortunately he doesn't explain what this involved, but it was enough to convince him. He wrote: 'An angel of evil could not have done that – it was the Archangel Gabriel.'

Because all the up-and-coming thinkers of Blake's day were rationalists, he was never popular or successful in his time – indeed, he was widely regarded as mad. And that, sadly, was what many people thought about visionaries for quite a few generations: that visions were evidence of mental instability, not to be taken seriously. But Blake believed that by imitating the angels in our lives and in our work, we can begin to realise our own divinity. Nowadays his genius is recognised and he enjoys a much higher reputation than he did in his lifetime.

3

Angels in Modern Times

The Nineteenth Century: The Angels Come Winging Back

Beauty and truth cannot be suppressed forever. Dictators throughout history have discovered that trying to control the human urge towards spirituality, music, art and poetry never works for long. After a few generations of virtual banishment the angels managed to effect a return with the help of Victorian thinkers and, especially, painters.

John Henry Newman (1801–90) was a well-known Anglican priest who later converted to Roman Catholicism. In 1833 he founded the Oxford Movement, which aimed to link the Anglican Church more closely with Catholicism. This movement encouraged people to bring colour back into churches, with the creation of new stained-glass windows and religious paintings.

It seems that the angels took advantage of this opening up of the imagination to inspire the artists of the time, especially the Pre-Raphaelites, who introduced many portraits of angels into their work. The Pre-Raphaelites, strongly influenced by Renaissance artists, depicted angels as youthful figures with bright halos, magnificent wings and long gowns. (Many of their paintings are reproduced nowadays on Christmas cards.) When people think of angels today this is often the type of picture that comes to mind.

One very beautiful painting by Edward Burne-Jones (1833–98), called *The Morning of the Resurrection*, depicts two angels sitting on Jesus' tomb, while the risen Christ speaks to Mary. All the characters wear very simple garments, made of pale-coloured linen draped into folds. The angels have very pale, almost translucent wings, and a light around their golden hair, which appears relatively short. On their foreheads are white flames.

Burne-Jones created many other angelic portraits, in stained glass and tapestries, which can be seen in churches and stately homes throughout Britain. By this time, the mid-19th century, people were beginning to enjoy greater freedom of thought and belief. The renewed interest in angels was accompanied by a general interest in psychic matters and mediumship – the British College of Psychic Studies was founded in 1884. People were beginning to realise that not all unusual phenomena could be dismissed as 'just the imagination.'

The Angels of Mons

The interest in spiritual matters that was growing through the beginning of the 20th century was encouraged by the stresses of the First World War. There was an increase in prayer and churchgoing, and many families who lost their young sons also looked for consolation in spiritualism. Was it this new openness of mind that enabled the angels to make their presence known? Because one of the most extraordinary events of the war was the reporting of a mass vision experienced by British soldiers.

There has been a good deal of controversy as to whether this event actually took place, and there are different versions of the event itself. Early in the war, vivid stories circulated in Britain about the soldiers who had been fighting against the odds at Mons, in Belgium, on 26 August 1914. The story began to circulate that the British had been helped by hundreds of armoured soldiers riding on horseback in the sky, led by a young man with golden hair on a great white horse, who looked like St George of England. The soldiers carried bows and were dressed like the men who fought for Henry V at the Battle of Agincourt almost exactly 400 years earlier in 1415.

Unfortunately, this version seems to have been based on a purely fictional short story published in September that same year, which was taken by some readers as fact and blown up into a modern myth. Disbelievers point out that no such happening appeared in army records.

There is another, less dramatic version, however, which sounds more likely and has more reliable supporting evidence. An English Brigadier-General wrote in his field notes that several men had reported seeing angels, and a lance corporal told the *Daily Mail* that he had seen 'a strange light' in the sky over the German line facing his battalion. In it, 'I could see quite distinctly three shapes, one in the centre having what looked like outspread wings, the other two were not so large . . . they appeared to have a long loose-hanging garment of a golden tint . . . We stood watching them for about three-quarters of an hour. All the men with me saw them . . .' And according to a German source, one of the German regiments found itself absolutely powerless to move forward at one point when ordered to do so.

Whatever the truth, something extraordinary happened at the Battle of Mons. The German army was much larger and much better equipped than the British, yet the Allied losses were much fewer than might have been expected. Moreover, the event opened up people's belief in angels, at a time when they were looking for spiritual support.

The Theosophists – Sowing the Seeds of the New Age

Meanwhile, an interest in less orthodox forms of spirituality had been growing. In 1895, some years before the First World War, a colourful Russian woman called Helena Petrovna Blavatsky had founded the Theosophical Society in London. Theosophy means 'wisdom of God' and Blavatsky wrote several volumes called *The Secret Doctrine* in which she describes the common thread which runs through all the great religions, stemming from the same roots of ancient wisdom.

The Society attracted a great deal of interest from men and women eager for spirituality unrestricted by traditional dogma. Some of its members were of high social standing, from academic and intellectual backgrounds – they included Annie Besant, who went to court to champion women's right to know about birth control. The Theosophical Society encouraged a growth of interest in the invisible realms and also in channelling. In 1936 a leading member, Alice Bailey, wrote *A Treatise on the Seven Rays*, which was based on channelled messages from a Tibetan ascended master and is still widely read by spiritual seekers. In fact during this period, the seeds were sown of much of New Age philosophy.

The theosophists demonstrated that angels, under various names, can be found in most spiritual cultures: all these invisible beings – angels, archangels or gods – are rays or emanations emerging from the Divine One, which divides itself into different aspects in order to build a variety of creatures. As the divine energy is sent outwards, all manner of nature spirits, devas, animals, plants, minerals and humans are formed, watched over by an army of light, which consists of solar and planetary angels.

Another famous theosophist, Geoffrey Hodson (1886–1983), was one of the first people to channel detailed and specific information about the angelic world, which he wrote about in several books. He describes God as a divine musician, conducting a celestial symphony in which all creatures are notes and harmonics participating in one great piece of music. One of his angelic encounters took place at Sheepscombe in Gloucestershire, in 1924, when he was meditating on the natural worlds. The sky became filled with an extraordinary radiance, which came into his consciousness; within the light he could see a beautiful and majestic heavenly being.

This god-like creature announced itself as Bethelda and gave Hodson a detailed description of the organisation of the Heavenly Host, and the relationship that angels have with humanity. Bethelda told him that if humans take time and patiently concentrate on the beauty of the natural world, we will naturally and easily perceive the angels, who are always there. But human beings need to take the initiative. The angels are ready and eager to work with us, but in order to build bridges between our worlds, more humans must be ready to play their part, and prepared to set aside time each day for angelic communication.

Geoffrey Hodson's book *The Brotherhood of Angels and Men* (London: The Theosophical Publishing House, 1982) describes different groups of angels – angels of healing, of power, of music, of nature and so on. To encourage our connection to the angels he recommends creating a sacred space, and the use of various colours: apple green for the nature angels, yellow for the angels of beauty and art, rose and soft green for guardian angels. Flowers, candles and beautiful objects should be used to create a 'shrine', which will help focus the mind when invoking the angels. All these recommendations are still valid, and I shall be returning to them in Chapter 5.

The Angel of Findhorn

The famous Findhorn Community in Scotland was founded in the 1960s by three friends who shared spiritual interests: Eileen and Peter Caddy and Dorothy Maclean. (Their story is told in The Magic of Findhorn *by Paul Hawken.)*

At the time they were living in caravans on a bleak Scottish camping site. Dorothy had been on her spiritual path for many years. She had worked with the Quakers, who understand the value of silence and inner wisdom; she had also worked with the mystical tradition of Sufism and had gradually developed her own spiritual gifts. When Peter Caddy set about trying to grow vegetables in the poor, sandy soil around the caravans, Dorothy was contacted during her meditations by nature spirits, who from then on gave the group guidance and explained what the plants needed in order to flourish. With the help of these spirits Peter grew 40-pound cabbages (cabbages usually grow to only four pounds or so) and other remarkably large vegetables. When members of the Soil Association visited them they were astonished; they commented that if people could grow food in the sandy soil at Findhorn, they could grow food in the Sahara desert!

Dorothy gave the spirits who communicated with her the Sanskrit name of 'devas' (beings of light). They explained that they were higher nature spirits, extending energy and protecting physical forms such as clouds, rain and vegetables, and in charge of smaller, individual nature spirits. Dorothy describes the devas as 'the builders of our world'; they continually transmute energy, which vibrates at high speeds as waves or particles, into the slower vibrations required to create physical matter. They carry the instructions of divine intelligence and help to build vehicles for the expression of life on all levels – mineral, vegetable and animal, as well as human.

Dorothy was also guided by a landscape angel, a being who overlit the whole area and told her that if humans cooperated with the spirits, wonders could be worked. The angel also gave Dorothy precise instructions about preparing the soil and compost, watering the plants and applying liquid manure. It continued to give the group practical instructions, but told them that the most important thing they could do to make the plants flourish was to radiate to them a sense of love and appreciation.

In addition, she has described how a new being, the Angel of Findhorn, gradually came into existence, 'gathering life from all of us in a new unity with mankind'. This angel 'grew phenomenally fast' from a kind of nebulous, sleeping form into a grand angel, fed by the growth of the magical gardens and the love of the human beings involved. This gives us an insight into the way human beings can cooperate with the Divine to help to create new angels, who will in turn assist the humans in their growth and development.

Today, Findhorn is a flourishing, world-famous spiritual community and teaching centre. Eileen, Dorothy and Peter did not set out with an ambitious vision; they allowed themselves to be guided along a path, without attempting to control the outcome. They worked with pure hearts and opened up connections with the devas for the benefit of us all.

Heavenly Hosts Greet the Cosmonauts

In 1985 an American weekly, *Parade Magazine*, published an extraordinary story. In July that year three Soviet cosmonauts orbiting the earth saw 'seven giant figures in the form of humans, but with wings and mist-like halos as in the classic depiction of angels'. The cosmonauts were performing experiments in the space station, *Salyut 7*, high above the earth, when they were enveloped in a brilliant orange cloud, which temporarily blinded them. When their eyes cleared they saw the angels, who followed them for ten minutes and then suddenly vanished. Twelve days later three more cosmonauts arrived on the space station and they also reported seeing the angels: 'There was a great orange light and through it we could see the figures of seven angels. They were smiling as though they shared a glorious secret ... within a few minutes they went and we did not see them again.'

The Hubble Space Telescope also picked up the orange light and NASA scientists thought they had received pictures of a new star cluster, because of the magnitude and brilliance of the colours. But when the computer enhanced the pictures they also saw

> seven angels flying together ... they were about 24 metres (80 feet) tall, with mist-like halos ... they had wing spans as large as aeroplanes. Their faces were round and peaceful and they were all beaming. It seemed like they were overjoyed at being photographed by the Hubble Space Telescope. They seemed to be smiling at each other as if they were letting the rest of the universe into a glorious secret.

Parade Magazine, 1985

Cosmonauts and other space scientists are trained in rational thinking and are not normally expected to have mystical experiences. In addition, the Soviet culture of the time was strictly atheist and would not encourage any of its citizens to use religious or spiritual language; so we can assume that they would not have released such a story if all the people involved had not been very convinced about its reality.

When I was a teenager, the first Sputnik went up into space and I remember people saying, 'Oh, well, the Sputnik hasn't found God up in the sky, so now we definitely know there is no such thing as God'. The story of the cosmonauts makes me wonder how many other unusual visitations there have been, which have never been publicised. In fact, there have been a number of rumours of angels being seen from aeroplanes and spacecraft, many reported by NASA astronauts. The fact that these reports rarely appear in newspapers may say more about the scepticism of editors than the reality of angels.

Angels and Near-death Experiences

Since the second half of the 20th century, and particularly over the last decade, a belief in angels has been becoming much more acceptable. Studies have been and continue to be made about people's experiences with angels. Among these, a good deal of research has gone on into near-death experiences, often referred to simply as NDEs.

Many people who have been very close to death have described encounters with angels and other spiritual beings. Deathbed visions have been recorded since antiquity, and the reports are always similar, whatever religion the person belongs to; even unbelievers have these experiences. Dr Raymond Moody started his research into these experiences in the 1970s and his book *Life after Life* was published in 1975. His findings helped to create a new approach to death and dying: nowadays more people are beginning to accept that death is not something to fear – indeed, far from it. NDEs are usually blissful experiences from which people are reluctant to return, and they nearly always involve meeting a being of light – in other words, an angel.

Making a Choice

I first heard about a typical NDE in 1972, before Moody's book came out; I had never come across such a story before, and it gave me goose bumps!

In the course of my work I met a woman called Barbara, then in her early sixties. She had lost her husband in the Second World War and had raised her two children alone. Not long after her husband died she herself became ill and was given an excessive dose of aspirin to bring down her temperature. At that point, she nearly died: she found herself going through a tunnel of light, where she was met by two shining beings who spoke very gently to her. They told her she could go on with them, in which case she would be reunited with her husband, but that she should also consider her two children, a boy and a girl. The light beings told her that if she went back to her children, it would be a very long time before she would be released from earth and meet her husband again. Barbara chose to look after her children, and returned to life. Just recently I heard that she had finally died when well into her eighties. She had waited half a century to be reunited with her husband.

The NDE often includes an out-of-body experience, in which a dying or very ill person seems to leave their body to find themselves above the scene, looking down at the other people trying to deal with the situation. This often happens with cardiac-arrest patients, who watch with interest as the doctors and nurses work to resuscitate them. Then they suddenly find themselves back in their body, often in great pain. The out-of-body experience has also occurred to people in car accidents and other crises. Sometimes an unusual helper arrives on the scene, to disappear when their task is done.

One of these stories appears in a book by Emma Heathcote-James, the first person in Britain to complete a Ph.D. thesis on the topic of angels. Struck by an American poll in which one in three people claimed to have seen an angel, she advertised for British people to come forward if they had had experience with one. Her book, *Seeing Angels*, is full of remarkable stories about angelic encounters, several of them taking place during out-of-body experiences.

The Gentle Helper

This story from Seeing Angels *is fairly typical: one man saw and heard someone who saved his life but later was nowhere to be seen.*

John Parkes was riding his motorbike when he slammed into a lorry. While his body was being tossed around, he found himself travelling upwards at high speed; from above he could see his body lying in a ditch. As he watched, he saw two people beside him, a man and a woman, trying to help, and heard a woman's voice calmly telling him to roll over. Suddenly back inside his body, he managed to roll over on his side, despite his broken arms, and resisting the male helper who was trying to roll him back and remove his helmet.

Later he learned that if he had stayed on his back or rolled the other way, he would probably have died. Later, too, he mentioned the woman as a possible witness to the accident – but no one else had seen a woman there. And afterwards, when he tried to remember what the woman looked like, his mind would go completely blank.

The Twenty-first Century – Angels are Everywhere

Before the advent of modern medicine, people rarely 'came back from the dead', and anyone who did was assumed to have been granted a special grace. Improvements in resuscitation techniques mean that many more people are rescued from near-death encounters and their stories help us to realise that spiritual experiences, including communication with angels, are available to us all. What we label 'New Age' philosophy really started with Madame Blavatsky, and since her day more and more people have chosen to follow spiritual paths that are not attached to any particular religion. This movement has gathered speed over the last few decades, and today many clairvoyants, healers and channellers have learned to trust the messages they receive from other realms.

Today, people are more open to supernatural occurrences, and the evidence for people meeting or being helped by angels is mounting up. Serious studies are being made of their appearances by researchers like Emma Heathcote-James, and organisations like the Alister Hardy Research Centre. People are no longer embarrassed about recounting their angelic experiences.

The Night-time Visitor

The following, very unusual story came from a young Australian man.

'I was lying in bed with my girlfriend; it was a hot night, and there was a light breeze. I felt ecstatic – so happy. It's hard to explain other than to say I felt loved for the first time in my life. My girlfriend was fast asleep. I was drifting off to sleep, then I remember just suddenly waking up. There was someone in the corner of the room. I was about to jump from the bed and attack them when I just sort of went calm and thought, "Oh, it's an angel." It's really hard to explain this because it sounds totally weird to me, but that's what happened. I watched him for a minute. It was a male, average height; you could see him but you couldn't really see any details. Then he looked at me and I knew he was surprised that I could see him, sort of like, "Oh, you can see me – clever."

'Anyhow, at that point he walked to the side of the bed that my girlfriend was sleeping on, and stuck his arm in her side. She sat bolt upright, and her right hand shot out and grabbed my left hand. She then rolled to the right to the bedside table with her left hand (a weird and difficult manoeuvre). Still holding my left hand, she picked a ring from the table and attempted to place it on each finger, one at a time, until she got it onto my little finger, which it fitted. She then returned to the horizontal position and went straight back to sleep.

'The things that make me believe that what I've told you is true are the following: first, the angel was wearing an American baseball-style cap – I despise them. Back then they were a rarity (1990–91), and if I'd made this up I sure as hell wouldn't have put a baseball cap on an angel; when the angel walked along the side of the bed it was as if the back of him was dissolving and being left in the air; he sort of floated and dissolved from the back, like wings but not like wings on a bird. The next day, when we got up, my girlfriend looked at me and demanded to know why I was wearing her ring! I exclaimed, "Hah! I knew you wouldn't remember," and I told her the story. She decided that I ought to keep the ring. Finally, even though I haven't worn the ring for years (I lent it to a later girlfriend, to keep her safe on a journey), on the little finger on my left hand you can still see where the ring was. It has faded a little into the other skin but it never tans, and if I get cold it is very distinct.'

There has been a huge change in mental attitudes and openness to spiritual experience. When I had my first angelic experience in 1974 there was really no one I could talk to about it. Twenty years later, when I channelled the messages for *The Angels' Script*, I felt that these would be worth publishing, and that people would accept them as valid and helpful. When one person develops a new possibility, then others find it easier – one man had to run the four-minute mile before other athletes could believe this was possible and follow suit. When Uri Geller demonstrated spoon bending, many people watching found they could do it too. And the people who found spoon bending the easiest were children!

There are many accounts of children seeing angels, while the adults with them see nothing at all. Children's minds are more open – they have not yet made decisions about how the world is; they have not created limitations, which block the gateways to other worldly beings. In the past children would be accused of telling fibs or told 'it's just your imagination'. Now that there are more adults around who are prepared to believe in angels, children who have these experiences will be encouraged rather than put down. This means that today's children are more likely to take their natural wisdom with them into adult life, which could make a lot of difference to the future of our planet.

There may be a number of reasons for the current increase in angelic visitations. Some people put it down to the ecological crisis our planet is suffering as a result of human activities, and believe that the angels are here on a rescue mission. I see this in a rather more positive light: the angels cannot help us without an equal amount of cooperation on our part. They are better able to communicate with us because people today are aware of our planetary responsibility and are opening up spiritually; this in turn is allowing the veil between us and the spiritual realms to become finer.

In the West, where most of our material needs are met, many people are finding that material satisfaction is not enough; ever since the 1960s more and more of us have been searching for spirituality not dictated by dogma. Angels provide a wonderful – and very practical – link with the Divine. As one angel expert has put it, the angels are like God's civil servants and when we need help, rather than bothering God, we can seek it from the right angelic department.

An angel is an invisible, highly charged vibration, which is able to move through time and space without the limitations we humans have to cope with. We can link our thoughts and intentions to the energy fields of angels, in order to create an effect of our choosing. And the more human thoughts are focussed on the intention, the more powerful the result seems to be. While it is true that some humans are naturally more able to focus their thoughts and make the invisible connections, this is a skill that can be developed by anyone.

Nowadays, people are discovering that they can tune into an appropriate angel for help with their problems, from small irritations to major issues. For example, when her cat refuses to come in at night, my friend Antonia asks for the angels of animals to give him a nudge – and this seems to work!

Help at the End of Life

A few years ago, Antonia asked the angels for help with a problem that was causing her a great deal of sadness.

'My mother, in her 70s, was terminally ill with cancer, but totally denying the fact, which made it very difficult to help her. She refused to contemplate going into a nursing home or hospice – she said she was going to live in her own flat until she was 90! The family wanted her properly looked after but we couldn't do it without her cooperation. I thought of praying, but God always seemed rather remote. Then I started reading about angels, and one night, when I was very anxious before a visit to her, I simply sat up in bed and said, "Look here, angels, I simply can't cope with this situation – please help!"

'The next day when I saw my mother, she said almost immediately, "If I've only got three months to live, I might as well spend my savings on a nursing home!" I was amazed. She had completely changed her attitude overnight and accepted the situation. After that we were able to talk properly about her illness and about dying, and make arrangements for her care. It just had to be the angels who got her to change her mind! We found a good nursing home for her, where she died fairly soon afterwards, very well cared for'.

The angels do respond. They can be called upon to assist with, or bless, just about any activity that is life supporting. But it is up to us to meet the angels halfway, and in the next few chapters I shall be showing you how to do this.

4

Preparing to Meet the Angels

In Chapter 5 I will be showing you how to meet your guardian angel, the first and most important celestial being in your life. You may be tempted to jump ahead in order to meet him as soon as possible.* However, your first experience of connecting to angels will be much more effective if you do some preparation first, and the techniques I shall be describing here will also help you to work in depth with the angels in the future.

In Chapter 1 I spoke about the four worlds, which vibrate at higher and higher frequencies the closer they are to the Divine Source. Mystical traditions speak of a heavenly ladder, which we can ascend, moving upwards from earth to heaven, meeting angels as we climb, and we can also think of the four worlds in this way. The fourth world, where we normally function, is at the bottom of the ladder. To contact the third and second worlds – the realms of the angels and archangels – we need to ascend the ladder by raising our mental and spiritual vibrations. We can do this through meditation and clearing our minds.

In this chapter I shall be describing a powerful way to meditate, using a mantra, which I teach people in my workshops before taking them on an inner journey to meet their guardian angel. I will also suggest some other techniques for preparing your mind, so that it is

---

* Angels of course have no gender, although some have distinctly masculine or feminine characteristics. For the sake of simplicity, however, I will refer to them as 'he'.

more open to receiving and transmitting messages from and to the invisible worlds; these techniques can be fitted easily into your everyday activities.

In the past, saints and mystics spent many years praying, meditating and fasting before they had major spiritual experiences. Nowadays so many people include meditation in their daily lives that it has become easier for everyone to move rapidly into spiritual realms. So don't feel you have to practise for months or years before you can move on – but do allow yourself some preparation time before meeting your guardian angel.

I suggest that you set yourself a date with this very important being, perhaps about a week ahead, on a day when you know you will have some quiet time to yourself. Mark it in your diary, just as you would a meeting with a friend. Then, during the preparation week, introduce some of the ideas included in this chapter, making sure you include the meditation. Think of yourself as a gardener who is putting down rich compost before planting out seedlings.

As we saw in the case of Antonia in the last chapter, if you have a deep spiritual longing to be in touch with the angels, the doors to the invisible realms will open to you, however busy or preoccupied you are. But in order to build a good working relationship with our invisible helpers, we need to open the inner doors of our minds. The great medieval mystic Dame Julian of Norwich said that God is like sunshine, but we put up our own shutters, which keep out the divine light. It is the same with all levels of the heavenly kingdoms. We have to allow a shift to take place; we have to draw back our mental shutters. Giving ourselves time to be at peace, creating a beautiful environment for our quiet times, chanting and singing or tuning in to inspirational music – all these will help us to move into those vibrational fields where the angelic work can take place seamlessly.

Clearing the Mind

The more you can re-educate your mind in new ways of experiencing creation, the more powerful your contact with the angels will be. Most of the time the human mind is very busy, often planning the future, sometimes regretting the past, but always chattering away to itself, leaving no space to hear messages from the spiritual world. You can think of your mind as a glass window on which all your busy thoughts have built up layers of dust, so that you are only aware of the surface and it is hard to see through the glass. Practising techniques to clean your mental windows creates an opening for the angels to look through, and also creates opportunities for your higher self to receive new information. In fact, clearing old thoughts and mental patterns is one of the most important processes for anyone on a spiritual path.

Not all our habitual thinking patterns are negative, but when you start noticing the small set of topics to which your mind usually returns, you will find many of them are based on fears and anxieties, worry about the future or regret about the past. So here are some techniques that I have found to be effective for my students and myself. Using the three Ms of mindfulness, magical awareness and meditation will help to clear your mind of clutter and enable it to become more finely tuned to subtle energies.

Mindfulness

This involves becoming aware of your thinking patterns during your daily activities. As you gradually become aware of the way your mind reacts to what's going on around you, you will begin to realise that your emotional responses to situations are within your own control: you will be able to choose how to react, rather than simply reacting automatically. You will then find yourself more peaceful and calm in situations that previously created anxiety and tension.

Here is a simple exercise that can be done at any time as you go about your day:

THOUGHTFUL ACTIVITY
Next time you are engaged in a task that does not require all your attention, such as washing up, ironing or cleaning the car (do not do this while driving), simply observe your thoughts as they come and

go. Allow yourself to become a witness to thoughts, rather than getting caught up in them.

Try it when you are washing up, for example. You may suddenly notice that you are thinking about all the other things on your list for the day. Maybe you are worrying about the time and what you have to do next. Maybe your mind is engrossed in other problems.

Bring your thoughts back to the present moment, paying attention to your immediate environment – the clouds in the sky outside the window, or a nearby tree. Be aware of the physical activity you are engaged in.

Allow your body to relax, even though you are still using your hands for the task. Notice how you are breathing – is there any tension there, because of some anxiety? Bring your attention back to the part of you that is a witness, and confirm to yourself that everything is as it should be. Here you are, doing your chores, and this is absolutely perfect. Even if you are concerned about time, you can say to yourself, 'Here I am, doing this job, and when I have finished I shall be moving on to something else.' Or, ' I can take my time, and do this work with love. If time overtakes me, I can finish it later.'

Taking this mindful, gentle approach to everyday activities creates beauty and stillness in our lives. Sadly the pressure of time nowadays means that many people have lost touch with the pleasure of carrying out simple, physical tasks. Practising thoughtful activity will help your mind to settle into a more restful state; your body will respond and you will find yourself dealing with everyday problems in a more balanced way. Once you start the process of witnessing your own thoughts you can take command, so that negative thoughts do not run away with themselves.

AFFIRMING THE GOOD

Becoming more conscious of your thought patterns will probably make you more aware of any habitual negative thoughts you have. Many people run a negative mental scenario throughout the day, maybe reliving old resentments, or mentally criticising themselves, without even realising they're doing it. Start to notice such thoughts, and see whether you can't change them.

For example, it's very common for people to be haunted by beliefs such as 'I'm not good enough', usually stemming from criticisms made in childhood. They are no longer appropriate to the adult self, if they ever were. People tend to take such beliefs for granted – but they may simply not be true. Once you recognise this, you can start changing them.

Our beliefs are very important; they provide a sense of safety and a structure for our lives. We couldn't sleep peacefully at night if we didn't believe that the sun was going to rise in the morning! But negative beliefs about ourselves and our lives limit our possibilities. Sometimes we have to make a breakthrough and shift our limitations, so that we can grow.

So next time you find yourself thinking something negative about yourself or your life, try to introduce a more positive statement – one that you can believe. For example, if you catch yourself regretting that you didn't do a particular job very well, you can truthfully tell yourself, 'I did my best'. Similarly, if you discover that you are still continuing an argument with someone you haven't seen for years, or resenting the bigger Christmas presents your sister got when you were small, you can tell yourself, 'That's past; now I can let that go.'

Another way of encouraging positive thought is through the use of affirmations. Affirmations were very popular a few years ago; many of my friends seemed to spend their time writing down statements they didn't believe, over and over again – rather like writing lines as a punishment in school. Writing something down over and over does not make it true.

I see an affirmation as a positive thought, which affirms that the possibilities in life are more likely to be good than bad, in the knowledge that the way we think about our life possibilities affects the result. Our thoughts, both negative and positive, are forms of energy, and the more powerful they are the more likely they are to produce an effect.

An affirmation can consist of a sentence such as: 'Life always brings me good things'. This simple idea can be introduced in your mind at any time when you notice your thoughts are becoming heavy. Or if you are anxious about your bank balance, you could try repeating to yourself: 'Money flows easily in my life'. If this sounds too unbelievable, create an affirmation for yourself that you can believe – for example: 'I am now open to receiving all the money I need'. (There are a number of good books on the use of affirmations; I can recommend Jane Duncan's *Change Your Thoughts, Change Your Life.*)

You can also use visual images to counteract a negative thought quickly. If you are feeling poor, try summoning up a mental image of your hands full of £20 notes! Or see yourself opening an envelope and finding an unexpected cheque for a large sum of money.

Statements and images like these can produce results, because affirming positive possibilities opens the way for the angels to act on your behalf, and helps their energy to create the changes you want. It is also important to keep reminding yourself that you are ultimately a divine being, that you have the power and authority to choose your own life. It can be helpful to find a statement or quotation that appeals to you personally. I use two lines from a poem by W. E. Henley to remind myself that I'm in charge of my own life:

> *I am the master of my fate*
> *I am the captain of my Soul.*

For most of the time we humans take ourselves far too seriously. By adopting a lighter manner, your approach to life will encourage your mind to open itself to the magical possibilities available to us all. Angels are light and innocent – as the humorous Catholic writer G. K. Chesterton has written: angels can fly because they take themselves lightly. If you allow yourself to become more playful the angels will be attracted to your lightness of heart.

St Teresa of Avila advocated the use of humour to dispel negative forces, and would shoo the Devil away, calling him a 'silly old goose'. One strategy I adopt when I feel negative thoughts getting in the way of my inner calm is to imagine them as little gremlins, with cross faces, rather like the gargoyles you find in churches. Then I mentally put them in a cage and turn the key. I find this quite effective. Not long ago I seemed to be doing this rather often, and realised I must have a whole zoo full of bad-tempered little gremlins! So I visualised my collection of cages only to find most of the little beasties had gone to sleep or melted away – out of boredom I imagine.

St Teresa also left us a very beautiful prayer, which I have often used in times of difficulty. Although I do not speak Spanish I say it aloud with what I hope is a correct accent:

Nade te turbe	Let nothing perturb you
Nade te espante	Let nothing frighten you
Todo se pasa	All things pass
Dios no se muda	God does not change
La paciencia	Patience
Todo la alcanza	Achieves everything
Quien a Dios tiene	Whoever has God
Nada la falta	Lacks nothing
Solo dios basta.	God alone suffices.

Magical awareness

Mindfulness is about noticing our own thoughts; magical awareness is about noticing the beauty of life, acknowledging the gifts that come to us every day and observing how often we receive just what we need, just at the right time. Here is something you could try:

SEEING BEAUTY EVERYWHERE

During your period of preparation, try for at least one day to see the underlying beauty in everyone and everything you come across. As you go to work on the bus, remind yourself that the bad-tempered bus conductor is also a spiritual being (even if he doesn't seem aware of it), smile at him and say, 'Bless you', when he takes your money. As you walk past derelict shops covered in graffiti, don't judge the teenagers who did the writing; send them a blessing from your heart and acknowledge that they, like all of us, have a divine spark – and often, artistic skill! As you wait on a busy platform for a train, allow yourself to see all the people coming and going as beautiful; practise seeing through their outer garments of stress and tension and open your heart to the divine light in each one of them.

And, of course, give yourself time to notice the undisguised beauty that is always around – the sunlight shining through leaves, the song of a blackbird, the colours in a flower or fruit stall. When you keep noticing the beauty in all creation, even the parts that seem hard to take, your mind can open to a new vision of life and become receptive to the invisible beings that are continually working to create beauty and harmony.

People are really surprised when I tell them that I have moved to London after many years in the country, but you don't need to live in a quiet place to develop your spirituality. One of my teachers pointed out that spiritual enlightenment is just as available in Piccadilly Circus as on top of a mountain. William Blake lived nearly all his life in London and he constantly saw angels.

Meditation

There are many techniques for stilling your mind that come under the heading of 'meditation'. Meditation allows the mind to discard its usual chattering activity and move gently into a quiet state, which encourages messages to arrive from our angels and guides. Regular meditation benefits the whole system; it allows the physical body to relax and the mind to become clearer as the constant jumble of thoughts melts away.

Meditation is a route back to your own soul, which is hidden like the sleeping princess in the forest, hidden by the brambles of our thoughts; our meditation technique provides us with a magic sword, which melts away the obstacles. The angels will also provide us with signs, encouraging us on the way, and the closer we get to the divine palace the more angels we will meet.

I started to explore ways to meditate when I was a teenager, over 40 years ago, and the most powerful method I have ever used is mantra meditation. It was after I learned transcendental meditation that I experienced the visitation I described in the Introduction. Ideally, it is best to learn this technique in a group with a teacher, since this provides an opportunity to ask questions and to be supported.

However, many people work successfully with mantras of their own choice and you could try this yourself. Do allow yourself plenty of quiet time for your first experiment, including before and after the meditation session itself. The day before you plan to work with your mantra for the first time, spend the evening quietly, avoid alcohol and rich foods, and give yourself a nice relaxing bath.

Treat your first session as a personal initiation and honour yourself by putting fresh flowers in your room and lighting candles. Allow yourself at least half an hour when you will not be disturbed – switch off the phone and muffle the doorbell. It is best not to meditate immediately after a meal, since your body will want to be busy digesting food, and the process of meditation encourages all the bodily functions to slow down.

USING A MANTRA

Choose a simple word, preferably of two syllables. It can have an appropriate meaning – for example, 'peaceful' – but also think carefully about its sound. Sounds that have hard consonants in them are not useful. Mantras given by yoga teachers will be chosen from Sanskrit, the ancient language of the sacred Hindu texts. These contain powerful vibrations, based on the simplest sounds we hear in nature, such as 'sssh', 'aah', and 'mmm'. Hebrew is another ancient language that contains these sounds, and you could try using the word *Shalom*, which includes all those sounds and also means peace. I use this mantra when I teach meditation in my groups.

Having chosen your word, you can begin.

+ Sit quietly in a comfortable chair that supports your spine in an upright position. Allow your hands to rest loosely in your lap. Keep your legs uncrossed and your feet squarely and firmly on the floor.
+ Your actual meditation time should be 15 to 20 minutes. Keep a clock near at hand, but don't set an alarm, unless it is absolutely necessary – in which case try to set it a good five minutes after you are supposed to finish meditating. It is not a good idea to be shocked out of a deeply relaxed state. You can peek at the clock at any time during the meditation. As you gain experience you will discover that you can set

your internal clock, just as you can 'set' yourself to wake up at a certain time in the morning.

+ Have a glass of spring water nearby, to sip when you have finished.

+ Start by checking through your body and focussing your attention on any tension spots. Say to yourself, 'Relax', 'Let go', 'This is my time'.

+ Allow yourself to observe your breathing. As you breathe, say to yourself, 'in', then 'out', 'in' and 'out'. Let your breathing become deeper and slower.

+ When you have settled into a gentle rhythmical breathing pattern, say your chosen mantra quietly to yourself. Keep repeating it to yourself, over and over, but gradually allow the repetition to be in your head, so that you are no longer using your voice. After this first session, it is not necessary to say it aloud; you can start off simply thinking your mantra.

+ After some repetitions you will probably find your mind wandering. This is quite natural; once you realise you are no longer repeating the mantra, simply start again. Don't try to force yourself into concentrating, but keep your attention on it lightly. You will notice that the mantra changes; it may slow down or speed up, or you may no longer know where it begins or ends. Then, after a while, the daily thoughts may trickle back in. When you notice them, return again to the mantra.

+ Gradually you will notice a deep stillness coming over your whole being. You may feel a sense of expansion beyond your body, and clarity in your mind that is like a bright light. This sensation is very blissful – I usually find myself smiling when it happens. It is a timeless experience in which you understand that who you are has no beginning and no end.

+ If this doesn't happen the first time you meditate, don't give up; your mind will eventually get the message. The most important thing is to take a light approach without aiming for mind-blowing results. Allow your meditation to be simple and easy, and accept whatever way it works for you.

+ When your meditation time is up, gradually bring yourself back to the room by wriggling your hands and toes, shrugging your shoulders, stretching and generally shifting your body back into action. It is useful to open your eyes slowly – look at the floor at first, so that you do not have a sudden influx of visual images.

I hope you will take time to practise this. It was this method of meditation that opened my own inner doors and allowed the angels to speak to me. I use this technique every day, at least once, usually twice. When I was expecting my last child, I practised an advanced version of it twice a day for a total of three hours, and also during labour, between contractions; my baby daughter was born with a blissful expression on her face, and she has had a peaceable nature ever since.

WATCHING THE BREATH

If you use a mantra you will notice how its rhythm begins to coincide with your breathing pattern. You can also meditate by focussing your attention on your breathing, without a mantra. Simply say to yourself, 'in' and 'out' in time with your breathing.

Simply observing your breath brings about a sense of being centred in yourself. If you consciously start to breathe more slowly and deeply you will find your body becoming relaxed and your mind clearing itself of everyday worries.

CANDLE MEDITATION

A candle flame is a magical dancing light. If you sit quietly with a lighted candle in front of you, watching the gentle movements of the flame, you will be drawn into a sense of peace and harmony. The presence of a flame lightens the atmosphere and gives a sense of well-being.

MEDITATION WITH MOVEMENT

Many spiritual traditions include physical movement as a meditative process, and this is particularly helpful if you are physically tense. Yoga is probably the most popular of these practices, and today an increasing number of people are taking up the Chinese practices of t'ai chi and chi kung, which use gentle flowing movements to align the mind, body, spirit and soul. It is best to work with a teacher: classes for these traditional practices are available in most places nowadays; even small villages often have yoga classes in their community halls.

WALKING MEDITATION

Walking meditation is something you can practise without having to go to a class. The rhythm of walking in itself allows your mind to sort out problems and issues; often you can set out on a walk with a sense of tension about something that is troubling you and return refreshed with a new perspective and clarity of thought.

If you set out on your walk with the intention of experiencing the present moment, always calling your mind back to the 'now', you will start to experience the world in a very different way. When you are aware of how things are, making no judgements about them, you see more deeply into the heart of creation. You can do this on a country walk, or even when you are doing the shopping. When I switch my mind into 'now' mode in the supermarket I often see auras around the other shoppers.

You can also try what I call 'deliberate walking', which involves very slow, careful steps, putting one foot deliberately in front of the other, heel to toe, very, very slowly ... how slowly can you walk? The advantage of this technique is that you can do it in a very small space, even round and round the patio!

Prayers, Blessings and Gratitude

Using prayer, blessings and gratitude as part of our daily life helps to prepare us spiritually, and we benefit from the wonderful sense of peace they give us.

Prayers

Through prayers, we send our silent or spoken requests for help from the underlying power of life itself, which some people call God, whether we send them directly or use an angel as a messenger. There is a reservoir of spiritual power, which is a resource for everyone to use, and when we pray we are asking for support from this realm, either for ourselves or for other people.

My brother is a scientist with no interest in spiritual matters, but when my mother was ill he mentioned having read the current scientific evidence showing that praying for the sick makes a measurable difference to their welfare. My brother did not want to think in terms of 'prayer', because he doesn't believe in God, but he was happy with the idea of 'sending positive thoughts'. These days, few people subscribe to the image of God as a bearded fellow in the sky, but most of us understand that there is a life-giving power that we can all connect with.

When we realise that the power of life is boundless, we can pray with a sense of certainty, knowing that anything we ask for is truly available to us – we are the only ones who put obstacles in the way of divine abundance. It is not so much a case of sending up a begging message, but of interweaving our own thoughts with the process of creation as it is unfolding. When we add our own requests to the existing angelic energies, miracles can happen effortlessly. There is a lovely tradition in the Jewish liturgy, which tells us that the Archangel Sandalphon collects the prayers of the faithful and weaves them into a garland, which is sent up to heaven.

Traditionally, people say prayers at bedtime and in the morning. Praying in the morning allows us to connect with the spiritual world, reminding us that underlying all the practical everyday things we are about to embark on there is a dimension of divine love that is supporting us. Praying at bedtime allows us to let go of our daily troubles, count our blessings and send love out to our fellow creatures.

Blessings

We use blessings as mental gifts to other people, which we send out through the invisible web of the spiritual world. When we send a blessing it is transported by angels – we don't have to know which ones.

We just need to think or say the blessing and a magical chain reaction takes place, transporting our positive desire to the right place. This means we can send blessings to people we don't even know.

A blessing is different from a prayer because it is sent with our own spiritual energy and, because it arises from our heartfelt intention, it carries a great deal of power. Empowered with our specific instructions, the angels will catch the blessing and carry it to its destination.

Gratitude

At the end of the day it's also helpful to review and give thanks for all the good things that have come our way. If you keep a spiritual journal, you can write them down – you may be surprised how many there are. Or you can get into bed and mentally count your blessings instead of sheep! 'An attitude of gratitude' is life enhancing and acts as a magnet for the angels to bring more and more blessings into your life.

Creating a Sacred Space

Very few people have enough space at home to set aside a whole room for spiritual work. But you can always create a sacred space in a quiet corner. I suggest you do this by setting up a special table, which will help to create a beautiful atmosphere however small your space. If you live with people who are not on the same wavelength as you, you can keep your angelic 'kit' in a special box, wrapped in a piece of silk. Then, when you have some quiet time to yourself you can make a ritual of setting up your space before beginning your spiritual work.

Obviously a quiet place is best for meditation and spiritual exercises – perhaps a corner of your bedroom. Try to ensure that it is not too cluttered with everyday stuff. As a general principle it is spiritually wholesome to do regular 'clutter-busting' in your life, and for angel work you want to have as few distractions as possible. Switch off the phone, hide away the daily newspapers or the children's toy-box – the sounds you hear, the things you see, should all be chosen carefully.

For your table, a piece of wood laid on a small box will do, or a shelf that is near a comfortable place to sit. You will need a cloth or a strip of fabric to cover it, candle holders, an incense holder and a flower vase. Anything else you include – such as crystals or pictures – can be collected as you go along, depending on what calls to you.

Using colours

Choosing the right colour for the table or tablecloth is important. Colours, like music, are very personal and what you are drawn to will often depend on your own responses. For example, although green is a life-enhancing colour, you may dislike it because it reminds you of school uniform. But deeper than personal responses are the collective responses of humanity, which are based on human reactions to colour in the environment. For example, golden yellow is the colour of sunshine, so we experience it as empowering, while green, the colour of nature and growth, is good for times of change. Particular colours are also connected with different archangels, and I will include these in Chapters 9 and 10.

The best colour to start with is one that calls to you. Often your 'favourite' colour when you were small is really important for your life. You may also change colours from time to time, depending on which angels you are working with.

Always use the best-quality fabrics you can afford – silk is wonderful and can often be found in Indian shops at very good prices. As you develop your work you may like to paint symbols on your fabric, which is easy to do with the excellent fabric paints on the market.

Using symbols

Symbols are simple images that help the mind tune into higher levels of understanding. You can include them in your space in many ways – you could create your own drawings; you could sew or paint symbols onto fabric; or you could purchase suitable items to hang on the wall. Symbols also carry profound meaning. The four directions of the Christian cross symbolise the fourfold nature of creation. The Egyptian ankh – a cross with a loop at the top– symbolises the everlasting nature of life. Both of these symbols are good for grounding.

The six-pointed star, known as the Star of David, is an ancient spiritual symbol. It is made up of two triangles, one pointing upwards to heaven, one pointing downwards to earth, symbolising the balanced union of heaven and earth.

Clockwise from top left: the Egyptian ankh; the Star of David; the Christian cross and the pentagram

The five-pointed star – the pentagram – symbolises the fifth element, which moves through all the worlds; it is sometimes described as 'a magical knot', because it can be drawn with one continuous line. (You can draw a five-pointed star in the air as a protection before and after spiritual work.)

I shall be introducing some angelic symbols in the Appendix, and you may discover others that work well for you.

Using flowers, candles, incense and essences

FLOWERS: everything that goes on your table should support you on your spiritual path. Flowers should be chosen for their colour, symbolic qualities and perfume. Some flowers are especially good for spiritual work – roses, lilies and jasmine are very special. As always, follow your intuition. If you can't afford a constant supply of fresh flowers, use pot plants, which last a long time, and also call you to nurture them. (Good-quality silk flowers can be used, but then it would be best to introduce some aromatherapy oils to provide a scent.)

CANDLES: night lights or candles bring moving light to your work. The flame symbolises the deepest part of your soul, where a divine light is always burning. Many churches and temples maintain a constantly burning light, and if you can do the same, even an artificial light will make a powerful contribution to your space. Knowing it is there while you are out gives you a sense of connection to your space, and returning to find the light still shining brings a feeling of certainty and strength. (Take sensible precautions about naked flames. Don't leave burning candles unattended or if small children are about.)

Candles can be chosen for both colour and scent. I like using tall dinner-table candles, which come in wonderful colours; I use different colours for different archangels. Night lights are useful – and very cheap – and can be left to burn in night-light holders. There are pretty glass holders available in many colours, creating different moods as you require them.

INCENSE: the ancients developed the use of oils and incense to a high art, and associated different incenses with different celestial beings. Many of these traditional incenses are not available nowadays, so for everday purposes I recommend frankincense, which is associated with Michael, the chief of the archangels.

Recently, some incenses have been created with fragrances that resonate with particular archangels, and you could try these out – but beware of those based on mixtures of many scents; simplest is best when working with the angelic worlds.

CRYSTAL ESSENCES, AROMATHERAPY OILS AND FLOWER REMEDIES: you can introduce drops of various essences, aromatherapy oils and flower and plant remedies into spring water or water from a holy well, and spray this in your sacred space to lift the atmosphere.

If you feel that the room needs cleansing, choose essences to clear it of difficult energies. Has someone recently had a crying session in your space? Or has a small child had a tantrum? Spray the room with spring water containing a few drops of Rescue Remedy. Essential oil of lavender is another good cleanser.

A number of essences have been created to resonate with particular archangels, and you could explore these. But in choosing them, use your intuition and be discerning – who has created them? Have the essences been developed from a base of love and service, or from a purely commercial point of view? At the back of the book I recommend some essences that I believe are made with integrity.

Using lustral water

I mentioned earlier that the angels in the Assyrian wall carvings are shown sprinkling people with holy water. This is called lustral water, which is used in ceremonies of spiritual purification. Although the word 'lustral' comes from a Latin word meaning 'to purify', this probably derives from an Indo-European word meaning light or bright. Using essences in a spray is a similar idea. You could also use water that has been blessed or collected from a holy spring or another source that feels special. After my first contact with celestial beings in 1974 I felt very vulnerable to negative energy. The Sufi friend who was guiding me told me I could create holy water myself to sprinkle around my house. All I needed to do was to put some water in a bowl and say a blessing over it.

You can create lustral water by leaving a bowl of water outside for an hour, either in the midday sun or under a full moon. Keep the bowl covered with clear film, which will protect the water from insects but allow the light to penetrate. Sunshine will create lustral water with dynamic (yang) energy; moonlight will create a receptive (yin) energy. Your choice may depend on what kind of work you are doing and which angels or archangels you are working with.

Using crystals, images and statues

CRYSTALS: many people like to use crystals for healing and other spiritual work. Crystals are passive: they receive and transmit the energy you send through them. I personally find that working with archangels is a more direct way to access different kinds of energy, so I rarely use crystals myself. But I do include a few when I am setting up a corner for a particular archangel. For example I have a white porcelain dish edged with gold, full of rose petals, where I stand a picture of Archangel Raphael; around the edge of the picture I have placed small pieces of rose quartz and amethyst, which I associate with Raphael's healing energy.

Your choice of crystals will depend on several factors: you may be drawn to a crystal purely intuitively; you may wish to use one that resonates with a particular angelic energy; or you may wish to create sacred corners for different archangels around your room, or around the house. I often set up a corner for Archangel Gabriel, the messenger, when I am writing or channelling. Then I will choose the appropriate colour for the candle, and introduce a suitable crystal and some flowers.

IMAGES AND STATUES: you can introduce all kinds of visual images into your space, including pictures of angels, and pictures or statuettes of spiritual teachers, such as the Buddha. Again, this is a very personal choice: you are bound to come across images appropriate for you at your stage on the spiritual path. And don't be afraid to create your own pictures, even if you don't regard yourself as a good artist. You can use collage techniques, using fabrics and cut-out paper, stuck with sequins and decorated with gold and silver angels or stars.

Using music and chanting

Sound is just about the most powerful tool for changing our states of consciousness. Spiritual traditions throughout the ages have used musical instruments for summoning celestial beings and for healing: the Jewish liturgy still includes the spine-tingling sound of the *Shofar* – the ram's horn – and the spiritual master Pythagoras healed humans and tamed wild animals with the sound of his lute.

The choice of music for your spiritual practice is another very personal matter. There are many tapes and CDs available nowadays which have been designed to accompany spiritual work; many of these use synthesised music, which I know people find very relaxing. But I would like to suggest that for angel work you find recordings using traditional angel instruments – flutes or other wind instruments, and lutes or other stringed instruments. There are also some beautiful choral pieces created by composers who wanted to lift our hearts and spirits. In particular, Mozart's descriptions of the way he composed suggest that he may have been channelling his inspirational harmonies.

There are no hard-and-fast rules, and you can enjoy experimenting. You may not always feel like gentle, ethereal music; at times you may prefer grand, stirring music that helps to charge your sense of power. I have found that some classical pieces of music resonate with particular archangels, and you may like to explore this for yourself.

Also available on tapes and CDs are chants; joining in with these provides a very uplifting way to begin a spiritual session. Again, you may enjoy doing some research and trying sounds from different cultural traditions. The angels we are working with have come through the Middle Eastern traditions and I find Hebrew and Arab chants very inspiring.

In addition, look out for recordings of natural sounds, especially water – the sound of a babbling brook or the sea has a profound effect on the mind, soothing it and allowing you to let go easily of your daily worries.

Don't use music while meditating with a mantra, or when you are going on a journey to meet the angels, but do use it to create an atmosphere in your space at any other time.

Using bells and singing bowls

Many traditions use bells in their spiritual practice, and the Tibetan singing bowls make truly magical sounds; if you can afford both, they are a wonderful means of producing a clear, singing sound in your space. Singing bowls can be used to clear the vibrations before you begin, while the 'ting' of Tibetan bells creates a powerful way to close your session.

PROTECTING YOUR SACRED SPACE

Whenever I am setting up a room for a workshop, I create four sacred corners for the archangels of the four directions – Michael, Raphael, Auriel and Gabriel – asking them to protect the space and encourage the spiritual energy to move freely among all the participants. You can do this when you begin a session at home, whether you are meditating or doing some other spiritual work.

If you are able to identify the four directions in your room – north, south, east and west – you can turn to face each corner as you speak. Start by facing south, then turn clockwise to the west, then turn again to the north, and finally to the east. If you have some cards with images of the four archangels you can place them around the room, in their appropriate corners. A lighted candle or night light in each corner is an optional extra – you can make these corners as simple or as elaborate as you wish, depending on how much time you have, and whether anyone else uses the room. You can also use incense and the sound of bells such as the ones that Tibetan Buddhists use in their temples.

Now invoke the archangels, speaking aloud and facing each corner in turn:

INVOCATION TO THE FOUR ARCHANGELS

I call on the archangels of the four directions to protect this sacred space and to assist me while I work.

I call on Auriel, archangel of the north,

I call on Raphael, archangel of the east,

I call on Gabriel, archangel of the west,

I call on Michael, archangel of the south.

I ask you to stabilise the four elements, fire, air, earth and water, to create a powerful base from which I can make my spiritual journey and to guide me safely on my way.

After your session, you can thank the archangels, mentioning each by name. If you have lit candles or night lights, blow each one out in turn as you thank the archangel and send the light to the appropriate corner.

Now that you have done some preparatory work by cleaning your mental windows and creating your own sacred space (even if only a small or temporary one) you can move on to a very exciting and important task – meeting your guardian angel.

5

Meeting Your Guardian Angel

The role of your guardian angel

Your guardian angel has been with you throughout your life, supporting and guiding you, even if you have been unaware of this. With every move you make, with every breath you take, your guardian is not so much watching you as *being with* you. Your guardian angel is a reflection, a spiritual twin, an image of who you will eventually be. I believe that your guardian was chosen by your soul many lifetimes ago, when you first made a commitment to spiritual growth. When your soul comes to its complete realisation of itself you will no longer need a guardian angel; he only needs to be there while you are still searching.

The most powerful way to evolve is through discovering the results of our own choices, and that includes making mistakes! Your guardian angel will not stop you making mistakes because they are an important part of everyone's life story. But he will provide opportunities for choice. It has been said that the earth is the only planet of choice: that is, that only on this planet do humans have free will, which is why so many souls wish to come here to evolve. (*The Only Planet of Choice*, compiled by Phyllis V. Schlemmer and Palden Jenkins.) The earth school can seem difficult, but it is only through difficulties that we discover more about our own spiritual nature.

Some of these difficulties can be extreme. I am often asked questions like, 'Where was the guardian angel when a child was abducted and killed?' This is a terrible thing to think about and brings up the issue of evil, which I will discuss at greater length in Chapter 7. The idea of karma can be helpful here. Karma can be described as 'the law of cause and effect', by which everything we do has an effect, whether this is good or bad. And everything has to be balanced, so we will keep being reborn until we have sorted out all our karma. This process is so complex, with so many layers building up over so many incarnations, that we cannot make judgements about tragic events, except to recognise that however terrible they may seem there will always be a spiritual meaning behind them. There is an essential logic to creation and it unfolds according to laws that we do not fully understand. What is essential is that we are not trapped into creating further negativity by allowing anger and the need for revenge to overwhelm our capacity for compassion. When we pray for lost children and their families, we must not forget that the perpetrators of terrible deeds may be more in need of prayers than anyone.

Before you were born, you made a particular agreement with your soul about this lifetime's journey. I have described how the four worlds of creation contain the hierarchy of celestial beings; because humans are part of the divine creation, we also have those four worlds within us, represented in the form of spirit, intellect, emotions and body. Your soul has come from the Divine Source, which is surrounded by the wisdom and love of the seraphim and has been nurtured and formed by the angels. Before coming to birth in a physical body in the physical world, your soul created a plan for this life with the help of the archangels. Your guardian angel was present when you made these choices, and is committed to help you honour your divine contract.

Guidance from Your Guardian Angel

Your guardian is also there as a guide to all four worlds, and can accompany you when you seek understanding from the celestial beings in these realms. He will act as your protector and your guide, and will provide you with a golden thread as you journey into their worlds.

So, before you attempt to work with other angels and archangels, it is essential to be in contact with your guardian angel.

Journeying through spiritual worlds is like setting off to sea: we need a navigator, some maps from those who have gone before us, a guiding star and an anchor. Your guardian angel is your navigator, and will also act as an anchor, enabling you to journey far and always come home again. Your guiding star is your soul's purpose for this life; you may not yet understand what that is, but your guardian angel will always try to bring it to your attention, in one way or another.

As for a map, when I take people on inner journeys I describe the route in some detail and always bring people back the same way, because the landmarks provide a sense of security and safety. This technique – of making sure you return by the same route you followed on the way out – helps you to ground yourself.

The Importance of Grounding

Grounding is essential to all spiritual work – it brings you back to everyday reality after working at a spiritual level. It's often tempting to stay in that pleasant, floaty state that you may experience during meditation or visualisation. However, the object of living on this planet is to express your spirituality through the physical plane, and you can only do that by ensuring that you come totally back to earth.

Grounding techniques include taking a symbol or talisman with you on your journey, making quite sure that you are fully physically present when you return, and writing or drawing your experiences afterwards.

Symbols and talismans

I mentioned some symbols in the previous chapter. You can hold one or have a picture of one by you before embarking on your journey. To return to the idea of going out to sea, you can think of the symbol as a lighthouse that sends out its light to keep you on course.

A talisman is a protective object; having a talisman with you for your spiritual journey provides a sense of place. It could be a favourite crystal, a beautiful pebble, a piece of driftwood, or perhaps a coin or a ring – anything that appeals to your physical senses, which is beautiful to look at or sensual to hold, and which will remind you that you belong on the earth plane. You can also use a shawl or blanket around your shoulders as a form of talisman. Ancient priests and priestesses both used shawls or cloaks to create a feeling of inwardness and solemnity. You can choose the colours according to your own intuition – you may wish to decorate your shawl with symbols.

Physical grounding

After any meditation or visualisation exercise, you should always ensure you are fully in your body. Wriggling your hands and feet, or doing some simple stretches, helps to bring you back to earth. If you are still feeling far away, get up and stamp your feet on the floor. You can also go to a window and take a few deep breaths of fresh air, or sip some spring water.

Your spiritual journal

Keeping a special book in which you note down your spiritual experiences and inner journeys not only provides you with a record of your progress but is also a good way to ground your experiences. Writing an account of your experience, or perhaps drawing an image of an angel you have met, brings the experience out of your head into the everyday world.

Choose a beautifully bound notebook book with plain paper inside, so that you can both write and draw in it, and keep it in your sacred space together with a good selection of coloured pens or pencils, including gold and silver. You could also have some gold stars

and angels to stick in when appropriate. Use your journal to record
your meetings with angels, your dreams, and any special occurrences
in your everyday life.

BEFORE YOU SET OFF

Many people nowadays use visualisations to explore the worlds of
the angels. Creative visualisation allows us to move into the world of
imagination, where we can call on the angels and archangels to
provide us with inspiration and guidance. And that is how you will,
in a moment, make your journey to meet your guardian angel.

The best way to do this on your own is to tape-record the section
below, so that you can play it back to yourself while sitting quietly in
your sacred space. Another possibility is to involve a friend who wants
to make the same journey: you could take it in turns to be the guide for
each other. This would be an excellent way to share your experiences
with a spiritual 'buddy'.

There is a point in the journey when you need some silence; this is
printed in capital letters.

Before you start:

✦ Switch off all phones.
✦ Organise your sacred space in the way that suits you best.
✦ Keep your spiritual journal handy, and any pens in colours you like
   using. Also have some tissues and some Rescue Remedy. Don't forget
   a symbol or talisman that you find useful for grounding.
✦ Prepare your sacred space with the Invocation to the Four
   Archangels (see page 76), by lighting incense and sounding bells.
✦ Take a few minutes to meditate. When you are calm, peaceful and
   relaxed, you can begin your journey.

TO BE TAPE-RECORDED OR READ ALOUD

Part A
✦ Observe your breathing, allowing it to settle into a gentle rhythm.
   Breathe deeply, breathe slowly.

✦ Imagine you are in a very beautiful sitting room. You are sitting on a comfortable sofa, facing glass doors that open onto a wonderful garden. In your mind's eye, you rise from the sofa and walk over to the doors. You open them carefully and step out into the garden.

✦ You wander through the garden, where the colours of the flowers and the dewy grass seem brighter than anything you have ever seen. You can smell the perfume of the flowers and the newly mown grass. You can see butterflies flitting among the blossoms. You can hear birds singing in the clear blue sky above you.

✦ As you walk slowly through the garden you come to a gate, which leads out of the garden. You open the gate and find yourself in a country lane.

✦ You walk along the lane. On one side is a hedge full of birds and little animals. On the other is a field of corn, with brightly coloured wild flowers – poppies, daisies and cornflowers.

✦ Eventually you come to some trees and find yourself wandering into a wood. The wood is quiet and you notice how the sun shimmers through the green and golden leaves.

✦ There is a path through the wood, marked with shining white stones. Although the trees are getting thicker, there seems to be a light ahead of you and you keep following the white stones until you come to a clearing, where the light comes from.

✦ In the clearing you find a shining building and you know that this is a sacred space, which has been waiting for you.

✦ The door of your sacred building is open and you sense that a welcome awaits you. As you walk inside you know that you have come home. The door gently closes behind you, to provide a safe haven.

✦ You find yourself in a golden room with a seat waiting for you. When you sit down you feel peaceful, happy and content. This is the place where you will meet and talk to your guardian angel.

Part B

✦ Ask in your mind: 'I now call my guardian angel to come to me. I would like to know your name and please tell me anything I need to know which is important to me at this stage on my life path.'

✦ Allow three minutes' silence at this point, so that you can talk to your guardian angel.

✦ Now say thank you to your guardian angel and get up from your seat. Move gently towards the door of your sacred room.

Part C

✦ You can still feel the presence of your guardian angel. As the doors open gently you step outside and start moving down the path of white stones, which guides you through the wood.

✦ Gradually the trees begin to thin out and you can see the sun shining through the leaves.

✦ You find yourself back on the path through the country. The hedge with birds and wild animals is on one side of you. The swaying golden corn and the wild flowers, scarlet poppies, white daisies and bright blue cornflowers are on the other.

✦ Eventually you find the gate that leads back into the garden, and you wander through the garden, smelling the flowers, and listening to the birds singing and the bees humming.

✦ You walk towards the house and step back through the glass doors into the sitting room.

✦ Walk back to the comfortable sofa and sit down once more.

✦ Before opening your eyes, breathe deeply and stretch your body like a cat. Shrug your shoulders and wriggle your hands and feet.

✦ You may need to take some time before you open your eyes. When you do, remember to look down at the floor first. Coming back into everyday reality should be a gentle process.

Now take your time to write down your experience in your journal, and draw an image if you wish. If you are with a friend, write everything down before sharing your experience with them. The process of writing sometimes brings more insight.

If you still feel slightly spaced out after writing, stand up and walk around, feeling your feet firmly on the floor. Eating a snack will also help to ground you.

Your experience

People experience this journey in many different ways, and whatever you experienced is valid for you. Some people find a temple like the Taj Mahal awaiting them in the clearing, some find a simple wooden hut, such as a hermit might use, or a small chapel. Grand or simple, this is a powerful space for you, chosen by a deep part of yourself as a suitable place to retreat to when you need answers to life's problems. You can go back to this space in your mind at any time. Use it as your inner, holy sanctuary.

Your guardian angel, too, may present himself in one of many different guises. You may see nothing, but simply feel a presence beside you, or just behind you. You may have an impression of a shadowy figure, or of a bright light. Sometimes people do see an angel with wings, but more often there is a sensation, accompanied by light and a feeling of joyfulness.

Some people do not get a response first time to the request for a name. This is fine – the name will come to you when it is important. One young woman on a workshop actually heard the name spoken in her ear – which made her jump! – but this is fairly unusual. And one of my students, who described the sensation of a silvery-blue presence, heard the name 'Alariel' as 'a high, fine sound, like a light breeze or a breath of sound'.

The impression is usually more mental. Some people are given ordinary names like Tom, or Jane, and that is also fine. Your guardian angel is a companionable sort of being, and will give you a name that is comfortable for you. Do trust this process. If he says his name is Tom, then use the name Tom when you call him.

My own guardian angel originally came to me as a bird. He seemed to be like a kestrel or a small falcon, and I could feel him sitting on my shoulder and occasionally lifting off and circling before returning. When he lifted away from my body, I could feel my soul lifting with him, and a physical sensation of lightness as though I was flying too. It was quite a long time before I discovered his name. I do find the name useful for bringing back my awareness to his presence. After all he is always there – I don't need to 'call' him – but using his name allows me to acknowledge his presence.

More recently, since I started to write this book, I have received a new image of my guardian, which is much more human, like a shining young boy. When I try to 'see' what he looks like, he is elusive, almost teasing, as though to say that I shouldn't try to force an image on something which is pure energy. He dissolves into light, and becomes transparent. There is a sensation of joy and delight around the presence of this energy, as though I am being encouraged to move into a new way of being.

Although birds or other creatures sound rather like the 'power animals' known to Native Americans, the guardian angel will appear in a way that is suitable for the person concerned, which may be in non-human form. When the poet Ted Hughes died, I watched a re-run of an old BBC Face-to-Face interview with him, which I remember vividly. Hughes described how he had a dream when he was at Cambridge, struggling with an academic essay. In the dream a large fox burst into his study and, standing on its hind legs, put its paw on Hughes's essay. 'This', said the fox, 'is killing us'. Hughes believed the dream was telling him to give up his English course – analysing literature gets in the way of creating literature – and he switched subjects.

Now, Ted Hughes had been brought up in the country. He was a down-to-earth man, probably not much given to thinking about angels. One of his most famous poems is about a fox and we can be sure that a foxy dream would be a more suitable vehicle for a message from his guardian angel (which is what I believe his fox was) than a visitation from a Pre-Raphaelite angel with wings and a halo.

In my workshops, some participants meet angels who give them a name of an archangel. I am sure that the great archangels do work as guardians with some people who are here to be of great service, for example as healers and spiritual teachers. But should you contact an archangel, don't let it go to your head: an inflated ego limits one's possibilities for fulfilling any important task. The ego is a very important tool, and we need it in order to develop a strong identity. But we should be aware that it is only a tool, and it should not be allowed to run away with a sense of its own self-importance. With a strong sense of our purpose we can achieve great things, and we should take our work seriously – but not ourselves!

The Imagination

Some people mistrust their experiences during the inner journey; since they have been asked to visualise, they feel that they've been 'making it all up'. And when I talk about my own visions, I am often asked, 'How can you know whether your visions are "real" or just your imagination?'

The imagination is the tool we use to translate the information we receive from the invisible worlds. Angels do not have material bodies that we can perceive with our ordinary senses; when they send us messages they are bypassing our everyday rational abilities and using our imagination to communicate with us.

We know that the left side of the brain uses reason to understand what's going on, while the right side of the brain is the vehicle for our imagination and creativity. Artists and poets are generally open to receiving information channelled through the right side of the brain; this is also the faculty used by mediums, clairvoyants and spiritual channellers. The information received in this way goes beyond the everyday stuff we pick up through our senses. Without our right-brained imagination we would not be able to translate the messages of the angels. And it is quite clear that the angels themselves are able to appear to us in ways that we can cope with; they have the power to give us messages through dreams, as voices in our minds or in visions, in such a way that we can understand them. Although those who are well trained in rational thinking may dismiss these experiences as 'only' the imagination, we have to decide for ourselves whether we can trust them.

Expect the Unexpected

Although people initially feel they are 'making things up', the images that come to them during their inner journey can be quite unexpected.

Eileen had been recently widowed when she came to one of my workshops a couple of years ago. She had been brought up as a Catholic but had left her faith when she married a divorcee. I got the impression that she thought I was going to be some kind of medium or spiritualist, who would put me in touch with her husband. She had a traditionally Catholic view of angels and guardian angels, and was obviously seeking solace and perhaps a confirmation that she should now return to her Catholic faith.

When Eileen shared her experience after the guardian angel journey she was obviously surprised by what she had seen – shocked might be a better word. The sacred building she found in the clearing was like a traditional church, with pews and stained-glass windows. But when she sat down ready to meet her guardian angel she saw a dark-skinned man in brightly coloured clothes, wearing a white turban fastened with a ruby brooch. He told her his name was Angelo and that she would have to go on a journey in order to discover something new. Eileen was amazed that she had not met the kind of winged angel she'd been brought up to expect.

A few weeks later Eileen phoned to tell me that the sale of her house had gone through; she now had her share of her husband's will and was able to make plans for her future. The first thing she was organising was a trip to India with a friend – previously Eileen's idea of travel had been an annual package holiday to Europe, so this was a big change. I felt that the extraordinary meeting with Angelo had shifted her perspective on life, and that she had opened her heart to all kinds of new possibilities.

What Next?

Now that you have made your initial contact with your guardian angel, you will find future contact much easier to make. This may not always be during a period of meditation or visualisation – you can talk to him mentally at any time as you go about your day, and he will respond. The response may not be instant, but you will recognise it when it comes. In fact you may realise that you have already had such contacts in the past. Even if you were not consciously seeking to communicate with your guardian angel, you can be sure that he has always had ways of contacting you. Messages can arrive in the form of a dream, or a meeting with someone who says something that rings true, or through an introduction to a life-changing book. And a well-known sign that your angel is around is finding a white feather, especially somewhere unlikely – indoors, or in a car, for instance. When you come across a white feather, it's as if your angel is saying, 'Hallo, I'm here.'

Even if your session with the guardian angel did not immediately seem to be a life-changing event, you can be sure that when you genuinely and sincerely seek a new relationship with your own soul your request will be answered. If you are not given a name when you ask for it, or some guidance for your life at this time, you may later have a dream which tells you more, or an interesting meeting or event will take place that will clarify things for you. Jesus said, 'Knock and it shall be opened unto you', and people who work with angels and are seeking spiritual development know this to be true. But you have to take time to listen to the answers.

Dreams

Ancient civilisations regarded dreams as a way for divine beings to send messages to humans. When we understand dreams in this way, we are encouraged to be open to our guardian angels and higher selves during our dream-life. Most people can recall at least one dream that has proved significant in some way, even life-changing – like the one Ted Hughes recounted.

Listen to Your Dreams

Margaret, who came to one of my guardian angel workshops, had a life-changing dream after her husband died.

In the dream, she met a cousin whom she had not been in touch with for nearly 40 years. When Margaret woke up, she felt that the dream had been telling her to make contact with this cousin. She did so, and the first telephone call she made led to the development of a strong new relationship between them. The cousin was involved in healing and spiritual work, and was able to help Margaret to see a fresh way forward in her life.

The more awareness you have of your dream life, the more useful your dreams can be to you as part of your spiritual development. You can ask your guardian angel for a dream to help you when you are facing a particular problem. It's useful to keep a notebook by your bed, so you can write down the dream while it's still fresh in your mind. You could also use your spiritual journal to double up as your dream notebook.

Asking for Help

You can send out a prayer, asking your guardian angel for help or guidance. Then be observant – there will be a sign, or a shift of some kind, and your problem may well be solved in some way you don't expect. It is most important to look out for and acknowledge any response – sometimes an answer will come, but we are often so preoccupied with the problem that we are hardly aware that we've received help.

USING A PENDULUM
One very direct way to get answers to your questions is to use a dowsing pendulum to converse with your guardian angel. For this you will need to buy a clear crystal pendulum, hanging from either a fine chain or a fine thread. Don't be nervous about your dowsing abilities; in my workshops I have never come across anyone who couldn't use a pendulum successfully. (If you want to know more about dowsing, I have recommended an introductory book in the Resources list.)

While you are still experimenting and growing in confidence with this method, I suggest that you meditate beforehand, so that you are feeling very connected to your inner world.

✦ Hold the chain or thread of your pendulum between your thumb and first finger, allowing at least 10 centimetres (4 inches) of chain or thread for the pendulum to swing from.

✦ Now ask the pendulum to give you a 'Yes'. The pendulum will move in some way, which differs from person to person. For me a 'Yes' is a clockwise circular movement, but for some people it is a side-to-side movement (which for me means 'No').

✦ Now ask the pendulum to give you two more indications, one for 'No' and one for 'Maybe'. Possible variations for the three answers 'Yes', 'No' and 'Maybe' include a clockwise or anti-clockwise circular movement, a side-to-side swing or a back-to-front swing.

✦ Always begin by asking the pendulum which movements indicate yes, no and maybe, because these can change between sessions.

✦ Now tell the pendulum you would like to talk to your guardian angel and ask whether it is all right at this time. Very rarely will it say 'No'. If you do get a no, please obey the instruction. It may be because you are asking from a state of anxiety and need to calm down a bit before trying again later.

✦ If the pendulum says 'Yes', you can begin a conversation with your guardian angel, using his name if you have it, and asking your question and receiving your answers via the pendulum. (You could actually use this method to find out the name, by going through the letters of the alphabet with your pendulum.)

✦ You can use the pendulum to ask for advice about decisions, posing any question which can be answered by yes, no or maybe.

✦ If you have to make a choice between several possibilities, you could ask your guardian angel for advice by writing the options down on separate pieces of paper and holding the pendulum over each one.

WRITTEN CONVERSATIONS

Some people find it quite easy to engage in a kind of correspondence with their guardian angel. Try writing down your questions, one at a time, and then immediately write down the answer that comes into your head, without thinking too hard. When I first used this technique, the replies came out in a quite different style of handwriting – my own writing was italic, which is quite sharp and precise, whereas the other writing was much more flowing. Over the years, my everyday handwriting has gradually become more flowing too.

Staying In Touch with Your Guardian Angel

By taking the journey to meet your guardian angel you have opened a portal, a door into another world, which is a deeper, hidden part of yourself. Rather like the children who stepped through the wardrobe into the land of Narnia, you have moved into the spiritual realms and you cannot easily turn your back on them. Once you have called them, the angels will be paying attention to you! If you forget to keep up your relationship with your guardian angel, he will find a way to nudge you or remind you – perhaps through your dreams or through a coincidence.

But the best approach is to keep going in and out of the door. Every time you meditate you can ask for inspirational guidance that will be useful to you. And don't forget to ask for help through the day when you wake in the morning, and say a quiet thank you at bedtime. Below is a bedtime prayer, which I find very powerful. This traditional Jewish bedtime prayer calls the four chief archangels to protect you while you are sleeping, and also brings in The Shekinah, the liberating angel who represents the hidden aspect of the Divine in humanity (there is more about her in Chapter 10).

BEDTIME PRAYER TO THE FOUR ARCHANGELS

May Michael be at my right side, Gabriel at my left side, Raphael behind me, Auriel in front of me and above my head The Shekinah, the divine presence.

When you get into bed, observe your breathing and allow it to settle down into a deep, slow rhythm. Then repeat the prayer very slowly to yourself. As you say the name of each archangel visualise a presence near you, to the right, to the left, behind and in front of you, as in the prayer. Then visualise a light above your head. As you go to sleep feel the presence of the four archangels and the light of The Shekinah surrounding you and enveloping you with protection and love, cradling you with infinite kindness. Sweet dreams!

One Hundred Blessings

In the Jewish tradition the pious person is obliged to say 100 blessings every day. These blessings are prescribed in their prayers, but I was inspired by this idea to see if I could find 100 things or creatures or people to bless each day! Sometimes I say them in my head as I am going to sleep … I don't often get to 100! You could try this as a meditation while you are out walking, saying blessings in your head as you walk, and keeping count on your fingers. When you are travelling to work, send out a blessing to anyone you see who seems in need. As we give so we receive; now try counting *your* blessings as well. I am sure you could quite easily find 100 blessings in your life.

Introducing Children to Angels

Young children are naturally very close to the angels and it is important to talk to them about the help they can receive from invisible worlds, especially in this sceptical age. We should never brainwash children with our own beliefs; but we can talk to them, listen to them, and encourage them to discover spiritual realms for themselves. We can help them to become confident, so that they learn to trust their own intuition, and follow any guidance that comes to them in dreams. It is very important to explain that an angel is not a person with wings in a white nightie, but an invisible power that can give them guidance and help if they pay attention. As the children grow, the education process invariably encourages scepticism and cynicism; you need to explain things in a sensible way so that the angels do not go the same way as the tooth fairy and Father Christmas as the child gets older.

You could introduce practical and inspiring activities so that your children have a sense of real involvement with the invisible power you are talking about. One idea might be to create a pin board where the children can put up photographs or the written names of people they would like to send blessings to. Suggest that they put these up in a thoughtful way, perhaps closing their eyes for a moment afterwards.

When my grandchildren come for a meal, I ask them to light candles for the table and to send a blessing to someone – they don't have to say this out loud. Recently my nine-year-old granddaughter Jane came to supper and she sent a blessing to her grandfather, who had recently died. As her parents do not have a spiritual practice and she had not gone to the funeral, I realised that this was probably the only opportunity Jane had for making a spiritual connection with her dead grandfather.

Another possibility is to get the child to carry out a 'scientific' experiment. Buy some cress seeds and plant them in two different trays. Then ask your child to give a blessing over one tray of seeds and to water this set with blessed water, treating the other tray in the usual way. Then encourage the child to keep checking which seeds are growing quickest. This simple, practical task invariably has good results and gives a child some 'ammunition' when talking to other, more sceptical children! It may also encourage them to use blessings at other times.

Many children these days are already highly attuned to the spiritual realms, and just need some encouragement and guidance. (It's also important to make them aware of the need for grounding.) My workshops are designed for adults, but when Vicky's mother rang and asked if her 12-year-old daughter could attend a workshop I was holding in Canterbury, I was quite happy for her to come on her own. The youngest person ever to come to one of my workshops, she was a dark-haired, sensitive girl, who asked some very insightful questions during the course of the day.

When Vicky asked for her guardian angel's name she was given the name Raphael. He also gave her some words, which she read to us afterwards:

> Dark and trustworthy,
> Fair and noble,
> Healer by day,
> Healer by night.

As she spoke these words quietly to rest of the group, the other participants seemed spellbound by the power present in such a young girl. Although the words were very simple, we all had a sense that Vicky was speaking from a place of strength and knowledge.

6

Manifesting Abundance

Now that you have made contact with your guardian angel, you can move on to connecting with other angels and with the archangels. In this chapter I shall be taking you through a five-part process, working with the four worlds and then connecting with the cherubim, which will help you experience more joy and abundance in your life.

One of the main reasons people become interested in working with angels is that they have a sense of inner lack. Many people in the West today are able to gather material possessions around them, and spend money on pleasurable activities, yet realise that there is something still missing. And what is missing is usually a sense of inner well-being and peace. Being in touch with the angelic realms naturally brings you into a state of peace and bliss. Trisha, one of my students, sent me this description of one of her experiences while working on the home-study angel course: 'I was asking for healing of heart and of emotions, for myself and two friends ... I felt expansive and connected in a clear, open and light way. I felt as if I were in a clear, soft, white space, in my heart *and* outside it.'

Joy and delight in living are available to us all, yet many people have become trapped into experiencing the world as a difficult place. I find that some people are suspicious if you seem to be 'in joy'; recently someone said to me, 'You're looking pleased with yourself; have you won the lottery?' I answered, 'No, I just enjoy being alive.' It's everyone's right to enjoy being alive. The lightness and peace that Trisha describes are actually simple to find, and the more we connect with angelic realms the more we will feel them in our everyday lives, not just during meditation.

Abundance

The wonderful word, abundance, conjures up a vision of endless supplies of everything! There is a rather puritanical notion that we should only ask for what we really 'need', not what we 'want', and that to ask for more than our basic needs is greedy. In fact, the universal energy is boundless and in the angelic realms there is no lack – which suggests that any limitations on our receiving endless supplies of everything have been set up by ourselves. This may be because we feel we don't deserve abundance. Quite often, however, we have set up our own particular limitations before entering this life, in order to develop our spiritual muscles by overcoming particular challenges. Limitation of one kind or another is part of our learning process. In the I Ching there is a hexagram called 'Limitation' which tells us that humans cannot cope with unlimited possibilities; without some limits our lives would dissolve into the boundless. The excessive behaviour of some rock and pop stars demonstrates how important boundaries are – excess is not the same as abundance!

What abundance really means is having exactly what is appropriate for you in your life at the present time. If you are a musician developing your talents, you will need a beginner's instrument; when you reach the level of Yehudi Menuhin a Stradivarius is totally appropriate. You may not be destined to be a Yehudi Menuhin, but every human has a purpose in the larger plan. Very often, though, people have lost touch with the reason they are here. So the first visualisation in this chapter is designed to help remind you of your purpose, by working with your guardian angel. Once you are clear about your purpose in life, it will also become clear what you need to support this purpose and you will be open to receiving what you need.

Working with angels to achieve your purpose will help you to become relaxed about life. You will find that things you once desperately wanted are actually not that important; you will discover that 'abundance' is a sense of freedom in which you know exactly what is right for you and are not drawn into wanting things just because the advertisers tell you that you need them. The philosopher Socrates is reputed to have said, while walking through a market, 'There are so many things I don't want!' He obviously knew what true abundance is. When you know who you are and where your life path is leading, then you will know exactly what you need and it will come easily to you.

Working with the Four Worlds

The four levels of creation described in Chapter 1 provide us with a simple and useful model of how things are manifested in everyday reality. The Divine Source (or God) starts the process by willing creation to happen. In the first world, the fiery seraphim surrounding the Source are like cheerleaders, with their constant affirmation: 'Holy, holy, holy'. In the second and third worlds the archangels start organising and planning and the angels get to work with the networking, making sure everything is looked after. In the fourth world the idea comes into actual being and the nature spirits, devas and humans protect and maintain it.

The process by which humans manifest what they need follows the same principles. Your own soul has come from the Divine Source with an idea of a perfect version of yourself. In the deepest part of your being the seraphim are whispering to you, telling you that you are also holy. Once you make contact with your own divinity you will become aware of your own innate, God-given power, which enables you to direct your life towards the perfection you have chosen. We cannot enter the world of the seraphim by using mental techniques, but you can ask your guardian angel to put you in touch with your own life purpose, and this will naturally connect you back to the Source. When we have established a real sense of connection with our own purpose, we will know exactly how to liaise with the archangels because we will know what we are trying to achieve. The archangels assist in the structuring of the plans that we create in order to fulfil our intentions. Then we ask the angels to support our plans by smoothing the way and attending to the finer details so that our plans will unfold effortlessly.

Perhaps you already have a sense of what you really, truly want to achieve; for example, many people who begin working with angels have already begun to train as healers. But others are simply getting along with life, finding a way to earn a living that doesn't feel too bad, even though it may not satisfy their deeper needs. And some may be in a situation that they definitely know needs changing, even without visiting their guardian angel.

Step One – Discovering Your Life Purpose

I am now going to take you on another inner journey, which you can make with the help of your guardian angel. This is a longer journey than the first, as you will be going beyond your sacred building. As before, either record this visualisation on tape or work with a friend.

TRAVELLING TO A STAR

The first part of the journey is exactly the same as the journey to meet your guardian angel, so please refer back to the previous instructions on pages 81–2 and record the words of Part A (up to and including: 'This is the place where you will meet and talk to your guardian angel.'). Then continue as follows:

✦ Call on your guardian angel, and ask him to give you insights into your life purpose.
✦ When you feel the presence of your guardian angel you find yourself being led to a shining staircase in the centre of the room. You move effortlessly on to this moving staircase, which carries you upwards. The ceiling of your sacred building opens up above you and the moving staircase takes you through clear blue skies, up and up, and through soft white clouds.
✦ Now the skies become darker around you, until you find yourself in

an indigo sky, full of stars. You are still being carried upwards on the shining staircase.

✦ Eventually you arrive at a huge shining star where you find a platform, which you step on to. Your guardian angel is still beside you and you are able to look down towards planet earth, a long way below.

✦ Now your guardian angel will show you highlights from your life so far, reminding you of any important people who have either helped you or who have given you life lessons.

✦ ALLOW TWO MINUTES' SILENCE.

✦ Next, your guardian angel explains why these things have happened. He is taking you back to the time before you were born, so that you can remember what you chose as the most important things you wanted to achieve in this lifetime.

✦ ALLOW THREE MINUTES' SILENCE.

✦ Your guardian angel tells you that your commitment and determination to carry through your purpose will be supported by the seraphim, the archangels and the angels.

✦ Now your guardian angel presents you with a symbolic gift, which will remind you of your purpose.

✦ You are guided back to the shining staircase and begin your journey downwards, towards the earth. You pass the stars in the deep-blue sky before moving through the white clouds and the blue skies and further down through the roof of your sacred building.

✦ Now you find yourself back in your sacred building, with your guardian angel still beside you. Thank your guardian angel and move towards the door.

✦ The rest of the journey home is identical to Part C of the first journey, starting from the words: 'You can still feel the presence of your guardian angel.'

✦ As before, make sure that you ground yourself on your return. If you wish, you can write down your experiences in your spiritual journal.

Don't be dismayed if you don't receive the answers you are hoping for all at once. When we are born we automatically begin to forget our divine purpose and sometimes this can take a lot of uncovering. I find that most people in my workshops do get something from this exercise; if it is not especially mind changing at the time, they may later report having a powerful dream. If you do not immediately receive messages, don't worry about it. Leave it for a while, and return to it when you have grown more confident about contacting your guardian angel in other ways. Remember, you can make the journey to the sacred building as often as you like, using it as a place of inner retreat where you can converse with your guardian angel and ask him to give you further insights. If you feel you need a clearer vision, you can revisit the star.

Remember, too, that whenever you work with your guardian angel you are making contact with all the four worlds within you and you automatically gain support from the seraphim, who surround the throne of the divine within your own soul. The seraphim fan the fire of your enthusiasm and passion for life, and whenever you feel low in spiritual energy you can invoke their power within by chanting their song 'Kadoish, Kadoish, Kadoish, Adonai Tsebayoth' ('Holy, Holy, Holy, Lord God of Hosts'). You can remind yourself of this sacred chant under all kinds of circumstances, not just when you are meditating. If you feel sensitive to negative energy when you are out and about, repeat it to yourself. These holy (wholesome) words can be used like a mantra that reminds us of the holiness of all creation – including ourselves.

Step Two – Working with Your Solar Archangel

As you become more certain of your own life purpose you can begin to make plans, so that your future activities will support that purpose. Once you feel more in touch with your direction you will find an energy and a passion arising in you that will provoke you into new action. But before you take action you need some support from the archangels.

Chapter 10 describes some archangels who can be helpful to you. They all have very distinctive characteristics, and you can choose to work with more than one, asking for help from any who seem appropriate for your life purpose. For example, if your goal is to become a healer you may well wish to work with Raphael, who is called the divine physician. If you want to make a public stand against the destruction of the rainforests, perhaps as an activist with Greenpeace, you could work with Hanael, who is a warrior archangel.

There are many, many archangels, all with different job descriptions. But from my own experience I find that the most important celestial helper you can connect with after your guardian angel is the archangel of your zodiac sun sign, your solar archangel. The reason why this archangel is so important is that your sun sign gives you the basic drive for this incarnation. The sun empowers your will to create and achieve your purpose, and the sign tells you what kind of purpose that will be. So before doing the following visualisation, look up your own solar archangel under your sun sign in Chapter 9. Then, as before, record the instructions on tape, unless you are working with a friend.

Before you start, write down the name of your solar archangel on a piece of paper in your most beautiful writing. Keep this paper in front of you while you are going on this journey. You could light a candle and put it beside the name of your archangel.

JOURNEY TO MEET YOUR SOLAR ARCHANGEL

✦ Ask your guardian angel to come with you on a journey to meet your solar archangel. Feel your guardian angel's presence beside you.

✦ Imagine you are in a huge, circular room. The walls around you are shining gold and set with crystals and precious stones.

✦ As you stand in the middle of the room you can hear beautiful music, as though choirs of angels are singing. Around the edges of the room is a series of 12 doors. Each door has different-coloured jewels set into it, and each has a name engraved in beautiful calligraphy. These names are the names of the solar archangels and you are looking for the door that has the name of your archangel on it.

✦ When you have found the right door you notice that it is opening gently and you see behind it a room full of light. You feel welcomed by the light and move towards it. You have the sensation of being drawn towards the light without any effort on your part.

✦ As you move through the door you are met by your solar archangel, who radiates beautiful colours.

✦ Now you can ask this archangel for guidance and clarity of purpose.
✦ ALLOW TWO MINUTES SILENCE.
✦ Now your archangel is presenting you with a gift. Thank him and say goodbye.
✦ You move effortlessly back into the golden room and watch the archangel's door slide gently back into place.
✦ Ask your guardian angel to take you back to your everyday world.
✦ Before opening your eyes do some stretches, wriggle your hands and feet, and breathe deeply.
✦ Now open your eyes slowly, before writing your experience in your journal.

Once you have established a real sense of contact with your solar archangel you can call on him whenever you are looking for support in planning your life. You can ask for help while meditating, or by using the pendulum or writing questions and answers, as suggested in the last chapter. If you want some everyday personal advice, I suggest you ask your guardian angel. If you are making a life-changing decision, you could ask both your guardian angel and your solar archangel. But if your question is specifically about your life's work, I advise communicating directly with your solar archangel. Regular contact with your solar archangel energises you and allows you to keep in touch with your purpose. My work with angels is a major part of my life purpose and I discovered my solar archangel, Saraquael, when I was channelling the messages for *The Angels' Script*. So now when I am making plans for developing this work I go straight to Saraquael.

Once you have an idea of your life purpose, and have developed your relationship with your guardian angel and your solar archangel, I suggest you do the following exercise.

WRITING YOUR MISSION STATEMENT

✦ On ordinary paper (not your spiritual journal at this stage) write down two or three sentences that describe your vision of your life purpose, which you have discovered by journeying to the star with your guardian angel. This is rather like a mission statement for a business: you are making a statement about who you are and what you intend to do with the precious gift of life. This is a general statement, rather than going into detail at this point; for example, 'I am here to learn about the many different cultures in the world and to help people to communicate and build bridges', rather than 'I want to travel to India', which would be secondary to this fundamental life purpose.

✦ Now write a list of actions you could take in order to further your vision. For example, if your purpose is to protect the natural beauty of the world, you might include joining Friends of the Earth, studying ecology at university, or becoming a volunteer for Trees for Life. If you want to become a healer, you could start by finding out the best places to train.

✦ Next, make another list of any things you may need to do, or to acquire, in order to further your plans.

✦ Now write down an outline of how you would like your life to work out during the next five years.

You may want to take a few days to consider your mission statement and your lists. Once you have started to think about them I am sure you will be presented with ideas. You might hear about something relevant on radio or TV, or read a magazine article, or come across information about a course at a local college. Now you have opened the door to your guardian angel and your solar archangel they will be directing you along a fast track. If you have recently been meandering along a side road, be prepared for a quick turnaround!

When you have a clear idea of your direction you may wish to copy your mission statement and lists, along with the five-year plan, into your spiritual journal (in your best writing, of course). Make a ceremony out of this, asking your guardian angel and solar archangel to witness your commitment. Then, with your mission statement and some basic plans drawn up, you can start working with the angels to help you put the fine detail in place.

Step Three – Calling On the Angels

The angels nurture us, creating a network of energy that helps life run smoothly. They help us with networking, making contact with the right people, finding the right place to live, and manifesting unexpected resources, including money, and – many people say – parking slots! They are very busy beings, constantly on the go. Someone in a workshop once asked me if angels ever sleep. I said, 'No chance! Too many humans making demands on them!' And of course, since angels do not have physical bodies they don't need sleep.

The angels' way of being is very innocent and simple. If something needs doing, they do it, without any of the hang-ups we humans have. They have a childlike approach to creating, and do not see problems. Because the Divine Creator supplies a boundless energy field in which every possibility can be created, the angelic approach will always be: 'It's easy', 'It's simple', 'Just let it be', 'Just love what is, create out of loving intentions, and all will be well'. This is the approach they encourage us to adopt so that we can work with them at this level. When our lives are based on love and spontaneity, everything runs smoothly; when we are blocked with fears and anxieties about the future we create energy fields that introduce difficulties, and life becomes tough to deal with. We can think of our thoughts as magnets, attracting abundance or difficulty, according to our mindset.

Although angels work lightly, do not think that their work is not serious. We must honour and respect their realms. The power and energy that can be activated when we ask angels to work with us is awe-inspiring. So, although it is not disrespectful to ask for help when you are stuck, do be aware that there are many things we can solve for ourselves. We shouldn't have to ask for help with a broken washing machine – but you can ask for angelic help in finding the right plumber! Networking and matching up the right people at the right time is just what angels are good at. When you work with angels, these synchronicities can happen very quickly indeed, and problems are often solved in ways we would not have thought of for ourselves.

Let's imagine that, after re-examining your life purpose, you realise that you have a mission not only to give healing, but also to teach healing. Perhaps you have already qualified with a reputable healing organisation, and there is a possibility of training as a tutor. This will cost money, and maybe you will have to find accommodation for weekend courses.

This is where the angels can help. The next task is to identify your exact needs – and there will be an individual angel for each one. In your spiritual journal use a fresh page to make a list of your needs – put the date at the top. For example:

+ I need £500 by 1 July to pay for this course.
+ I will need somewhere to stay in London for four weekends over four months. I don't know anyone in London.
+ I will need someone to feed the cat while I am away. My neighbour has cat-phobia so I've never asked her, and I am not sure who else I can ask.
+ Now close your eyes and send out a prayer to the angels for what you need. Since you've made your needs very clear, a general prayer is probably good enough, but you could say specifically: 'I am asking the money angel to bring me £500 to do this course', 'I am asking the bed-and-breakfast angel to find me somewhere to stay – free!' and 'I am asking the pet angel to find a cat-loving person to feed Fluffy.'

How long will it take to get a result? The answer to that question is 'How long is a piece of string?' Because we are human and tend to think everything needs planning and organising weeks or even months in advance, we expect the angels to need plenty of notice. But I have the feeling, based on years of experience, that angelic magic works best when a quick turnaround is desirable. There is an immediacy about angelic energy – if you give the angels a long deadline they will take as much time as you give them, and you may not get results until the very last minute, while you sit there wondering whether you have been heard. This is not a deliberate ploy to keep you on tenterhooks. It is just that pure energy acts in the now, not in the future. In the angelic worlds the future is unfolding as it should, from moment to moment. The more you work with angels the more you will learn how to allow this to happen in your own life.

Angels also work on the principle of 'divine economy' – they like to solve as many problems as possible in one move. For example, at the last minute before your first weekend course, you could have an unexpected call putting you in touch with someone in London who needs her tropical fish fed while she is away, on exactly the weekends when you need somewhere to stay.

Divine economy may also lead the angels to sort out the finances in a way you had not expected. The deadline is approaching, there is no sign of the £500, and you are beginning to fret, but you then make enquiries and find out that the organisers of the course are prepared to accept four payments of £125 over the four months of the course. Often this kind of discovery is preceded by an angelic prompt, almost like someone whispering in your ear 'Why don't you phone the organisers and explain your situation?'

Exchanging messages with the angels

I mentioned earlier that a general prayer for what you need is good enough for most occasions, and there is also nothing to stop you mentally speaking with your guardian angel or any other angel while you're on the bus or in the bath. However, there are some delightful ways to leave messages for the angels that bring an element of playfulness into your relationship with them. Doing something that brings fun into your life helps you become lighter in your spirit, and this attracts angels like a magnet. Here are some suggestions for some angelic ways to send messages:

MAKE A MESSAGE BOARD

Use a small pin board – you can get plain ones quite cheaply. Collect sparkly fabrics, pretty paper and some feathers (many craft and gift shops sell feathers in angelic white or beautiful colours). Some gold paint would be useful too; use this to paint the frame of the pin board. Decorate your board to become your angel message board, on which you can pin requests for yourself and for other people. When you have visitors invite them to pin up their requests as well.

CREATE A LITTLE BOOK OF ANGELIC THOUGHTS

You may not think you are a poet, but angels will often send you beautifully worded messages, which you can collect and refer to whenever you need your spirits lifted. Find a small book with a beautiful cover; mine was hand-made in Tibet from recycled paper that has rose-petals in it. Whenever you receive an inspirational thought from the angels, write it in your book, using coloured pens, with a touch of gold and silver. Once you have organised the book you will probably receive lots of messages; angels are good at filling empty spaces!

WRITE A LETTER TO AN ANGEL

Write letters to angels, asking them for help – for yourself or for others – or thanking them for their gifts. Make each letter as beautiful as possible; embellish it with stickers or little golden angels. Decorate the envelope as well, and make the letter look really special, like a wedding invitation. You can put the letter in your sacred space; or thread a ribbon through one corner of the envelope, fix a feather to another corner, and hang it in a window like a dreamcatcher. Or simply carry the letter with you until you find somewhere that inspires you as the right place to leave it – maybe hanging from a tree, or in a church.

MAKE PICTURES

Before most people could read, images of spiritual beings acted as windows for connecting them to the invisible worlds. There are many pictures of angels available as birthday or Christmas cards. There are also some packs of angel cards for spiritual guidance. Or you could create your own picture; even if you don't think you're a great artist, you can easily make a picture of an angel, using collage techniques. Find old cards, magazines, pieces of beautiful fabric, gold and silver doilies, coloured feathers and some of that sparkling glue that comes in many colours. Take some time in your sacred space to play with your materials; allow the process to be intuitive and do not rush to add to the image.

USE LITTLE BOXES

I love leaving messages for angels in little boxes. There are lots of magical-looking boxes available quite cheaply, especially in shops selling handmade products from India and the Far East. I like writing on really pretty paper. Sometimes I write the message around the edges and put a symbol in the middle of the page. Or I write in a spiral, starting in the centre and writing round and round until the paper is full. Then I fold the paper up really small and put it in the box – sometimes I put a small piece of crystal in with the letter.

The Perfect Home

The first time I discovered that leaving messages in boxes worked was really by accident.

About 20 years ago we were living in Somerset, near Glastonbury, and we needed to move house to somewhere smaller and cosier. In order to be clear about exactly what was needed, I wrote everything down on a piece of paper, stating the number of rooms we wanted, and specifying that we needed a garden. I didn't think of this being a message to an angel or anyone else, but I did fold the paper up and put it in a small box. Then I forgot all about it. Not long afterwards, when I was taking my baby for a walk, an old country woman leaned over her fence and asked me whether I wanted to rent one of her cottages. I had quite forgotten about the piece of paper. It was not until many months later, after we had moved house, that I came across the box. When I read the paper inside it I was amazed to realise that the house we had rented exactly fitted all the requirements I had listed. This was my first experience of the direct power of manifestation. From this lesson I discovered that the more precise you are about what you need, the quicker the result. Nowadays I address my little letters to the angels – sometimes by name – before putting them into boxes.

Whatever method you use to send messages to the angels, do keep a record and remember to acknowledge the angels when you receive the support you asked for – even for parking slots! And, at the end of each day, thank them for all the things you have received that day, many of which you may not have consciously asked for.

Step Four – Working with the Fourth World

If you work harmoniously with the angelic worlds, the people, the things and the money you need will start to flow easily in your life. There is an old Sufi saying: 'The path is smooth, do not throw rocks in your way.' Letting go of fears and anxieties helps to smooth the way ahead. Meditation and a commitment to experiencing the beauty of life bring about an inner peace, which allows everything in your life to flow seamlessly.

When you begin to realise that what you need does manifest easily, please honour the gifts you receive. Not only should you acknowledge the help you get, but you also need to play your human part as steward of the physical world. If you ask for a better car, or a new bike, and receive just what you asked for, then your job is to look after the gift – keep the car clean, or your bicycle well oiled. Angels help to bring the right people together, and can help you to manifest useful physical objects, but the next step is a human task. If you meet a good contact at an event, it's up to you to make the follow-up phone call. If you are offered a second-hand cooker just when you need one, don't expect an angel to appear with rubber gloves and clean it for you!

Humans are also stewards of the natural world, and we have many invisible helpers – fairies, water sprites, elves and pixies as well as the grander nature spirits, called devas. They exist in the fourth world, and, although it is hard for most people to see them they can be seen by people who work closely with nature. All these magical beings are happy to work in collaboration with humans who are creating beautiful gardens, replanting forests, clearing disused waterways or growing food. They are often known collectively as 'elementals' because they assist with the process of manifestation, encouraging and maintaining growth in the natural world, which consists of the four elements. The Greek philosophers tell us that there are four groups of elementals: salamanders – fire; gnomes – earth; sylphs – air; undines – water. You are likely to feel an intuitive connection with one group more than the others, depending on your temperament. Your astrological chart can also indicate which element is strongest for you.

MEETING NATURE SPIRITS

Here are some suggestions to help you get in touch with nature spirits, or elementals:

Dryads

These are the spirits of trees and woods – I suspect the green lady seen by the young man in the wood in Chapter 1 was a dryad; you may see one yourself if you spend plenty of time communing with trees.

✦ Find a very old tree in your locality – if you do not live in the country, try your local churchyard, as they often have ancient yew trees growing in them.

✦ Sit quietly at the foot of the tree, leaning your spine against the trunk. Allow your breathing to slip into a gentle, quiet rhythm.

✦ Ask the spirit of the tree to communicate with you. Allow yourself to feel the power and energy of the tree and stay quietly with it. Notice the effect the tree energy has on your mind, body and spirit. Perhaps you will become aware of the tree speaking to you in the form of thoughts arising in your mind.

Finding the Spirit of the Tree

Paul, one of my home-study students, tried this exercise and sent me the following description.

'I chose a yew tree close to an old church tower. At the time I was feeling sad, and I noticed that its powerful and benevolent presence uplifted me and that my heart grew lighter. A robin starting singing beautifully a mere three feet away, almost as a welcome!'

Fairies

These beings are notoriously difficult to spot! When I was small I was always on the lookout for them, especially on moonlit nights. I often had impressions of sudden movements of light, but I could never be sure quite what they were. However, I did get the feeling that they like to tease human beings. But there are certain places where, and certain times when, they are more likely to be seen.

✦ If there are woods near you, go there very early one spring morning, while the dew is still on the ground and before other human beings are out walking. Be prepared to wait quietly and patiently and send out your messages to the fairies as thoughts or whispers. Tell them you are prepared to work with them – all invisible beings are drawn to willing humans. You must make it clear that you have a genuine desire to connect with them, and are not merely curious.

✦ If nothing happens, send them another message telling them you will be back. Persistence and patience invariably produce results, and you may be rewarded by a glimpse of a tiny light being.

Most people I have spoken to who have seen fairies say that the encounter happened unexpectedly, and that the fairy looked as surprised as they were. People also report that they are often glimpsed at the edge of vision, not always seen full on.

Elementals

Decide for yourself which of the elements you have most affinity with and create a situation in which you may commune with the elemental. Here are some ideas:

✦ FIRE: the best way to commune with salamanders – the elementals of fire – is to build a fire yourself. A bonfire out of doors or a good log fire in your own fireplace would be ideal. Sitting with the fire, and feeding it, perhaps for several hours, will allow your own spirit to be filled with fire energy, which is healing and energising. Watching the leaping flames, gold, red and electric blue, you will feel drawn into the power of fire, and may even see the spirits moving as they transform the wood into a new energetic form, releasing light and heat. Listen to the fire: it makes its own music. Perhaps it calls you to feed it with incense, which releases an inspiring aroma. As you look into its depths, the salamanders may bring you visions – the famous medieval prophet Nostradamus used fire to scry the future.

✦ AIR: a visit to a hilltop is essential for communing with sylphs, the spirits of the air. These spirits are especially elusive and you will experience their activities only through their interaction with the natural world. Watch the grass rippling in the breeze. Watch autumn leaves twisting and turning. Gather a bunch of dried leaves and release them into the wind, sending love and blessings with them as they drift away. You could even write your blessings on the leaves before you let them fly. The sylphs will also carry your voice. When you stand on the hilltop you can call out this Buddhist blessing to the four directions, turning to face each direction as you call – do not be self-conscious, use your voice as loudly and clearly as possible:

> *Peace to all beings:*
> *Peace to the east,*
> *Peace to the west,*
> *Peace to the north,*
> *Peace to the south,*
> *Peace to all beings.*
>
> *Joy to all beings:*
> *Joy to the east,*
> *Joy to the west,*
> *Joy to the north,*
> *Joy to the south,*
> *Joy to all beings.*
>
> *Serenity to all beings:*
> *Serenity to the east,*
> *Serenity to the west,*
> *Serenity to the north,*
> *Serenity to the south,*
> *Serenity to all beings.*

> *Love to all beings:*
> *Love to the east,*
> *Love to the west,*
> *Love to the north,*
> *Love to the south,*
> *Love to all beings.*

✦ WATER: undines are present wherever there is a natural source of water – in streams and rivers, in lakes, in the sea and in rock pools. Artificial water features in your garden will also attract their energy. But close contact with the sea – walking on the seashore, paddling in pools, or swimming – is one of the most powerful ways to make contact with the flowing, healing energy of undines.

In Greek mythology the water spirits are called naiads, and they are renowned for creating beautiful music; listening to the sounds of water will change your energy in remarkable ways. Listen to the sea moving, or water tumbling over pebbles. If you cannot get to the real thing, there are recordings of these sounds available.

Many people have found that swimming with dolphins is a transformational experience and I am sure that the spiritual quality of dolphins and undines is very similar – the spirit of water is inclusive and nurturing; it removes our sense of separation and allows us to accept the unconditional love of the universal spirit.

✦ EARTH: in order to keep yourself well grounded while developing your angel work, you must be sure to keep in touch with the hardworking gnomes, elves, dwarves and pixies. Creating a space for yourself to be physically in touch with earth is really important. Since I have been living in a top-floor flat, I have noticed how my energy shifts when I go down to street level. From my window I look down on a very pretty garden, but walking on the grass in a local park makes me feel physically centred.

Apart from digging a garden or tending a window box, a good way to contact earth elementals is by communing with stones, pebbles or crystals. Dwarves and gnomes have a reputation for working with precious minerals and metals. There is plenty of good literature on working with crystals, and you do not have to become an expert to use those that appeal to you. When you are out walking, look out for stones or pebbles that attract you, and bring them back to your sacred space. Or find a natural outcrop of stone in your locality, where you can sit and feel the energy coming up from the deep earth.

Connection with earth energy is especially important when we work with angels; it helps to keep us grounded and prevents us from getting out of balance. We need to keep in touch with all the elements in order to be complete and whole.

Step Five – Asking the Cherubim to Watch Over Us

The cherubim are the most powerful beings we can call on. They are able to connect energy through all the four worlds and their purpose is to maintain creation and to keep everything in balance. In the Jewish tradition there is one particular cherub sitting on the throne with God, who can take on every form of angel, bird, beast or human. The human form of this cherub is the model for God's creation of humanity. This story reminds us that, unlike the seraphim, archangels, angels or nature spirits, we humans have access to all four worlds through the spirit, intellect, emotions and body. The cherub symbolises the 'quintessence' – the fifth element, which maintains the unfolding processes, making sure nothing gets out of balance. The creative process goes through four stages, and the fifth holds everything together, like spiritual glue. According to Jewish legend, when King Solomon needed help sorting out the demons, the Archangel Raphael gave him a five-pointed star, symbolising the power of five to bind the fourfold process of creation.

The cherubim have a special role as protectors. In the Bible we find the Israelites being given very specific instructions on how to make a sacred casket, the Ark of the Covenant, in which to keep the stones inscribed with the Ten Commandments. Once created, the Ark was protected by golden figures of winged cherubim.

Although we are unlikely to meet the cherubim, we too can ask them to watch over what we are doing and create a protection for ourselves. When I close my meditation I draw an outline of the five-pointed star in the air, while repeating a Hebrew blessing: 'Baruch attah, Adonai,' which means, 'Blessed art thou, oh Lord.' Other symbolic gestures of protection could include putting a ribbon around your little box, or around your envelopes containing letters to the angels, saying a blessing at the same time.

Finally, here are some lines from an old Irish invocation for protection, called St Patrick's Breastplate:*

> I stand in strength as I stand today
> With the hierarchy of the Cherubim,
> In the willingness of the angels,
> Under the wings of the archangels.

(* Translated by Jay Ramsay in *Living Christianity* by Martin Palmer, Shaftesbury, Dorset: Element, 1992)

7

Co-creation

D id you know that human beings help to create angels? Tradition has it that the angels have always been there, created by God before humans came along, but this is only partly true: new angels are being created all the time. The Jewish mystical *Book of Creation* (the *Sefer Yetzirah*) tells us that there are two kinds of angel – permanent ones and temporary ones. The temporary angels were created first, because the permanent ones had to wait to come into being with the stars; they are considered to be the souls, or intelligences, of the stars.

The permanent angels have names and are as numerous as the stars in the heavens. But troops of temporary angels are still created every morning as part of the continuous process of creation. Mystical wisdom tells us that creation is ongoing: when we understand that we ourselves are part of the creator God, then we can start to realise that we are helping to create angels, as well as communicating with existing ones.

We are unconsciously participating in the creation of angels all the time – through our thoughts, our wishes, our intentions and our prayers, as they link with the consciousness of the creative process. In this chapter we will be looking at the conscious co-creation of angels. They may be temporary ones, as when we ask an angel to find us a parking space, or they may be longer term – for instance when we appoint an angel to help us with a major project. We saw in the story of the Angel of Findhorn (see pages 45–6) how the intentions of the people involved in creating a garden from a dead landscape awoke a latent energy, which grew into a great angel, at first 'still nebulous, though growing phenomenally fast'. We are told that they 'gave it strength from the depth and dedication of our activities as we aimed for perfection' (Dorothy Maclean, *To Hear the Angels Sing*). In the same way, our own intentions and energy can help to awaken angelic energies to bring more abundance into our lives.

What Co-creation Means

Co-creation means that our thoughts and actions contribute to creation – we are not just the puppets of the old-fashioned God, the great 'clock-maker in the sky'. These days many of us understand God as an active energy, a process rather than a fixed being, with which we can consciously collaborate. And when we introduce the idea of co-creation into our spiritual language we can take more responsibility for our part in the way our lives develop.

The idea of co-creation is very popular nowadays, but it is not new. A famous Jewish mystic put forward this radical view of our relationship with God nearly 500 years ago. Isaac Luria (1534–72) suggested that God is a creator who is still in the process of discovering His own creation, and that humans are participating, helping to bring forth the highest possibility. God shares consciousness with humanity, and both need to work together to realise the full potential of that consciousness. There is an element of struggle in this because God's consciousness, or spirit, from which creation flows, is unbounded, whereas the material creation has to be placed within the boundaries of time and space. Often our own spirit finds it difficult to be contained in matter and we resent being limited. But when we realise our co-creative power we understand that boundaries are useful tools for creating what we desire, and then we may discover that the material world is our playground.

Working with angels puts us in touch with our creative possibilities. The more we work with the angels and realise that we help to create them, the more we discover who we really are – divine beings, with boundless energy, who have chosen certain limitations in order to create a world full of beauty and abundance. Remember this idea: that we have *chosen* our own limitations. If we want to re-negotiate our choices, we have total freedom to do so.

Creating Our Reality

The stuff from which creation is manifested is pure, unformed energy, and this energy has consciousness, which invents certain basic patterns or formulas. Within our universe there are some patterns that are fixed, which can be calculated by physicists and mathematicians, but within the limitations of these fixed laws there are endless possibilities. I think of the archangels as being in charge of these basic patterns, from which the angels work to develop a multitude of beautiful possibilities.

Everything in creation has within it divine intelligence and energy – rocks and minerals, trees, flowers, humans, animals – and angels. We humans have a high level of self-consciousness and we are beginning to learn how our thoughts help to create the events of our lives, and even the physical world. Since thoughts are forms of active energy, our negative thoughts lead to negative outcomes and our positive thoughts lead to positive outcomes. So we are always participating in creation, whether we are aware of it or not. As we grow in consciousness we begin to understand that this is not only true some of the time, but also that it is constantly true. Every thought instantly initiates a train of events, even if we don't realise it at the time. And the more spiritual work we do, the more aware we become of the powerful effect of our thoughts.

So, every morning when 'God' sends out new troops of angels, you are helping 'Him'. You cannot help participating, since you are a part of the whole. Since we are all part of God, we are naturally involved in sending out troop after troop of angels, all with their instructions. In order to become more skilled at co-creation, we human beings need to fine-tune the way we function at all levels – spiritual, intellectual, emotional and physical. For without self-awareness, our thoughts can have consequences we may not intend: not only do they help to create the angels, but they also can help to create negative entities. So, before I offer suggestions for creating angels, I would like to say something about the 'dark' side of creative power.

Co-creating Mischief and Chaos

When the energy of consciousness flows smoothly, the end results are harmonious. The collective consciousness of humanity has manifested amazing beauty in music, in art, in gardens, in architecture; it has also invented wonderful technological gadgets that support human life and make it more comfortable and enjoyable for many people. But we also see, every day, the results of human indifference and wickedness. We see the results of dreadful weapons of destruction, and we are learning that famine, caused by floods and droughts, is a direct result of humans interfering with the delicate balance of the ecology of the planet. We have abused our co-creative powers, largely because we do not understand just how powerful we actually are. We are entitled to be creative, and make changes to the way things work naturally, but this must always be done with respect and love, seeking only the highest good for the whole.

When our thoughts are negative, based on fear and guilt, we contribute to a pool of negative energy, which creates a chaotic force field. This force field becomes a reservoir from which negative entities manifest themselves and seek to promote more negative thoughts, in order to maintain their own existence. Sometimes people feel 'invaded' by unwanted negative thoughts, over which they seem to have no control. When people are ill, especially if they are depressed or generally unhappy about their lives, if they are low in self-esteem and feel unloved, these dark entities can latch on to the sadness, fear, guilt or anger and amplify it. So long as the negative force field is growing, the entities will be mischievous and disturbing, but we can easily disarm them by invoking angelic forces. The angels are able to take the negative energy and convert it for a higher purpose.

The pure energy of consciousness is not in itself 'good' or 'bad'. It simply gathers into patterns, which are set up by the vibrations of thoughts. If a negative force field gathers a huge amount of energy, fed by the fears and anxieties of humankind, then it manifests itself collectively in what we call 'evil': in murders, racial hatred, wars and genocide. Often people who support what turns out to be a terrible political regime are ordinary, well-meaning folk only wanting the best for themselves and their country. They have just not looked deeper, thought more carefully and/or responded more immediately; 'evil' is able to grow rapidly because of this general lack of awareness and the refusal of many humans to take personal responsibility.

Lucifer and Satan

The issue of 'evil' has been a thorny problem for philosophers throughout the ages, and especially for theologians trying to explain how dreadful events could be allowed by a benevolent and all-powerful God. One of the most terrible myths which has been handed down through the ages is the story of a prince of darkness, ruler of a terrifying place called Hell. He has been given many titles but is best known as Lucifer or Satan.

The name Lucifer means 'bringer of light', and was used by the translators of the Bible as another title for the 'day star', the planet Venus. The myth of Lucifer as a rebellious angel who was cast down from heaven is based on a misinterpretation of the biblical text. It was the early Christian Church that developed the idea of Lucifer as an evil prince of darkness who became the ruler of Hell. It is quite clear, however, that the ancient biblical prophets believed all the angels belonged in heaven: there was no separate place called Hell. The Jewish teacher Jesus would not have recognised the idea of a separate, demonic power, with its own dark kingdom. Such a place, ruled by an evil overlord, would have to be somewhere where God had no power, an idea that is incompatible with an all-powerful and omnipresent God. Nor is a place of eternal punishment compatible with a loving God who wishes the best for all of us.

The same applies to Satan: although Satan, or the Devil, is a very real figure to some people, he or it has actually been created out of negative thought patterns and beliefs, and can therefore be disempowered by positive thoughts and energy. The Hebrew word 'satan' means 'adversary' or 'tester', and in early Bible stories God sends angels as satans, to test human beings. In the story of Job, this God-fearing man is put through terrible tests by the angel Satan, but always with God's permission. It's worth remembering this whenever you find your life full of difficulties. Perhaps you have co-created a satan for yourself, who is testing your resolve and working hard to put you on the right track. The satans who turn up in our lives are messengers from the divine part of ourselves; every test calls something to our attention and asks us to examine our motivations and intentions. A famous Christian saint, Augustine, once said that the so-called bad angels exist in order to give us something to resist, so that we can become more virtuous.

It is worth understanding the origins of Lucifer and Satan, in order to diminish the idea that evil can have power over us. Any power the 'Devil' has was co-created over the centuries by human thoughts, images and fears, and can be dissolved with angelic help.

Preparing to Co-create with Angels

When you begin to co-create with angels, you need to be peaceful and centred. This is why meditation is so important. You cannot create something good for yourself if you are anxious and full of doubts. Lack of self-worth is a chief cause of difficulty; it can lead to a host of nasty little gremlins in the back of the mind, which manifest as resentment of others, fear of failure, or the projection of difficult scenarios preceded by 'what if'. If you already have a pattern of creating discomfort in your life, it may seem hard to believe in the possibility of co-creating something beautiful with the help of the angels. The most important thing to realise is that you have been actively involved in creating your own life – it has not just happened to you: you are the prime mover, the captain of your ship. If you want to steer your life in a new direction, you need to identify your true purpose and work with your guardian angel to clear negative issues. Then you will be able to start the process of co-creation with a light heart.

Co-creating New Angels

There are plenty of angels already available for us to work with. According to the Talmud, 'For every blade of grass there is an angel saying "grow, grow".' Anything that has already been created, by nature or by human creativity has an angel. You can be sure that there exists an angel for pets, an angel for your local library and hospital, an angel for the aeroplane taking you to your holiday destination. But when people start to create something new, a new angel comes into being, as with the Angel of Findhorn. And when you choose to create something new in your life, you can call on angelic energy and consciously 'grow' a new angel.

The more meditation we do, the more our own creative power increases. This is because meditation allows us to get in touch with our own divine power; during meditation we can touch the source and sing with the seraphim. Then we begin to understand in a very clear way exactly what we are here to do. With a clearly defined mission we can be unstoppable! St Augustine tells us that when the angels set about doing something nothing stands in their way; this is because they do not have human self-doubt or emotional hang-ups about success. When we get in touch with our own sense of purpose, we can also leave self-doubt and anxiety behind us and set about manifesting our heartfelt desires. So, step one is to make sure that our co-creation programme is based on desires that make us feel enthusiastic and intensely committed – a fiery passion about our projects is the foundation stone on which we build our creations.

The next step is to consider our project: what is involved, who needs to be consulted and how much it would cost, if anything. For example, you might be planning a new kitchen. In this case you will need to do measuring and costings, consult various kitchen companies, check your DIY catalogues and look at the various options. This step is a mental project, and you can ask the archangels for help – identify which archangel would be interested in a new kitchen! I would choose Cael, archangel for the sign of Cancer, who nurtures home and family. Then there is Baruel, archangel for Scorpio; Baruel is interested in cookery, because it involves an almost alchemical process of transforming basic ingredients into wonderful meals. And Orphiel, archangel for Capricorn, would be helpful in making decisions about the structure and layout of buildings and rooms, as well as helping with the financial possibilities – such as gauging whether this project will increase the value of your property. (You can find more about these zodiac archangels in Chapter 9.) The archangels will also help you become emotionally detached about the financial side, allowing you to see your project as a creative task with a series of problems that have to be solved; you will gradually understand that a problem can be solved in more than one way.

The key to this stage is to maintain a vision, empowered by your connection to the source, but to be open and flexible in visualising exactly *how* it will come into being. It is a seriously bad habit of most humans to give up on their desires because they cannot see how to achieve them. Working with the angelic realms allows us to create visions and become confident that our thoughts and wishes will eventually manifest, perhaps in ways we have not thought of, so long as we keep faith in our own worth and in divine love.

After you have collected all your thoughts, you can write down a plan in your journal. First identify your mission; for example:

'I want to create a beautiful new kitchen, with plenty of light, which will be efficient to work in but also cosy and welcoming for family and friends. I want the kitchen to be ready before the festive season, which is nine months away.'

Then write down the various stages you think have to be achieved:

✦ Do we need planning permission to extend from the back of the house?
✦ If we can extend, how much more space can we create? Get measurements.

✦ Find magazines and brochures with kitchen ideas.
✦ Get costings from architects and kitchen fitters. Explore DIY kitchens.

Find out about sources of finance – the bank, parents, etc. At no stage allow yourself to get anxious about finance. One of my students, a single mother on a low income, wanted a new kitchen but had no idea how this could be managed. But, after working on house improvements for some time, she had become aware that if she asked for help, sooner or later something would manifest. It did when she was phoned by a kitchen company offering cut-price kitchens (last year's designs) and her mother generously offered to foot the bill. If you don't ask, you won't get anything. (But be careful what you pray for, they say, as you might just get it!)

Now that you have everything as clear as possible, you can create angelic help to achieve your plan.

BRINGING A NEW ANGEL INTO BEING

✦ Start by meditating in your usual way and follow this by visualising the new kitchen in as much detail as possible.
✦ When you feel you have a clear vision of the future of your project, visualise a small seed of bright light.
✦ Focus this light in your mind at the centre of your forehead, behind your third eye chakra.
✦ Say that you will dedicate your own energy to the project and ask the light seed to participate and grow into an angel who will support you and any others involved. (The more people who are consciously supporting the project, and tuning into the angel, the more powerful the energy will be, and the better the results.)
✦ Ask your growing angel to help by bringing what you need towards you.
✦ Practise this visualisation daily, after your meditation.

When the kitchen is complete, you could create an Angel of the Kitchen picture to hang on the wall. And don't forget to invite the nature spirits in, by introducing growing plants such as herbs or decorative houseplants in hanging baskets. Take time to thank the angel for its help, acknowledge all the people who have supported you: you could stand in the kitchen and speak your thanks aloud. You could invite all your human helpers for a dinner party! And make an inner commitment to take proper responsibility for the practical maintenance of your new kitchen.

This is a very practical example, and plenty of people already create good things for themselves in a similar way, without being aware that angels are always in attendance whether or not their help is consciously asked for. However, you could apply the same principles to creating a project that is less straightforward to achieve. A project like the Findhorn garden might seem much more difficult to pin down, since there are so many more factors involved – and at Findhorn money played only a tiny role. Even so, each small developmental step showed the early settlers there how to work with 'the laws of manifestation' and it was made very evident to them that a clear vision is needed to lead to a speedy result.

For example, they wanted a new garden shed. They had been thinking about it and asking for it for some time and nothing was happening. Then they realised that no one had any kind of idea how big the shed should be, what kind of wood it would be made of, whether it needed windows, and so on. Once they wrote down the details, a donation of exactly the right amount of money quickly arrived. (David Spangler, *The Laws of Manifestation*.)

If you are working on a project that involves people, such as setting up a healing group, you can use the same basic principles. First, set out your vision, then identify what is needed, such as a room once a week (angels are good at helping to find free premises for voluntary work) and enough responsible, trained people to offer the public a healing service that they can trust. You will also need to check on practical matters like insurance and so on. In this case, once the healers are gathered together they could work jointly to create the angel for their healing project, and then work with the angel individually between meetings.

Developing Your Confidence

As you experiment with these ideas, you will find yourself more and more able to relax about your life, knowing that the divine power within you is able to co-create all your material needs. And remember that 'needs' are not about having just enough to get by: divine energy is boundless, and working harmoniously with the celestial worlds will bring joy and abundance into your life, so that your cup will overflow. Ask for what you truly desire from your heart and it will come to you. Just be sure that you are prepared to take responsibility for the material goods that you receive, that you share generously, and that your values do not become lopsided.

THINKING ABOUT YOUR LIFE

Here are some important points to think about as you develop your confidence in co-creating:

✦ Consider what you think. Meditation will help you become observant so that you will begin to notice when negative thoughts arise and will be more able to change them.

✦ Consider what you eat and drink. Not only can we enhance our own emotional, physical and mental well-being by avoiding animal products and processed foods, but also we can reduce the amount of suffering which is a direct result of using the animal kingdom for food. In addition, some foods are only available to us because people in underdeveloped countries have given up growing crops for their own families. Wherever possible be alert to this kind of exploitation and buy products from ethical companies.

✦ Consider what you wear. Simple, comfortable garments allow us to move freely. Natural fabrics allow the body to breathe, and garments made by loving hands are wonderful; they may be expensive, but remember that very cheap garments are often created in factories that exploit their workers.

✦ Consider what you say. Language and sound have spiritual qualities. Sounds make vibrations in the air and create connections between us.

Angry, critical words invariably have hard, aggressive sounds, while loving words are *soft* and *gentle* – say those two words aloud and you will hear what I mean. Remember that if you cannot say something nice about someone, it is better to say nothing at all!

✦ Consider where you go and how you get there. Do not be afraid to go into busy places; the angels are with us always and everywhere. But think of your own quality of life. Being pushed around on an overcrowded bus every morning will not help you arrive in your office feeling calm and clear headed, and driving a car contributes to pollution and congestion. But walking and cycling are both energising and good for the body.

✦ Consider your interaction with the natural world, understanding that we are collectively responsible for the future of our planet. Commit yourself to being a good steward of worldly goods and remember the old adage – waste not, want not.

✦ Consider how you use your time. Balance the hours in your day between concentrated work and relaxation, exercise and fun. When you begin to bring abundance into your life with the help of the angels, you will find the difference between work and play diminishes. Even so, spiritual traditions encourage us to take real time out, for one day a week – a holy day, or Sabbath. This allows us to evaluate the previous week and create our intentions and visions for the time to come. We can also avoid all those busy-busy activities that make life so stressful. Spend time with friends and family; visit places of natural beauty, or wonderful buildings. Or, stay at home and luxuriate in a bubble bath, ask your partner for a massage, play silly games with children – leave the phone off the hook! Whatever you have been missing because of the demands of work, allow yourself time for on your holy day – wholly for you.

This may seem like a lot of 'considering', but this is not meant to be hard work. The word 'consider' means 'to be with the stars' and, remember, there is an angel for every star in heaven. We do not have to live like monks and nuns in order to lead spiritual lives and we should not be ashamed to take pleasure in the beauty of our planet and the beauty of human creations too. But we will find we enjoy our lives much more, and feel more connected to the angels, if we simplify the practicalities in our lives and find delight in natural beauty and loving relationships. Remember that we are co-creating in *all* our activities.

In order to co-create successfully, and with integrity, we need to begin with a heartfelt, passionate intention. We need to consider our vision from as many angles as possible, allowing it to take shape in more detail, and ask the angels to help by drawing helpful people and assistance towards us. Finally, we have to take responsibility for the care and maintenance of the natural world, including our own creations and possessions. Most of all, we can delight in participating in such a wonderful world and enjoy contributing our own creations, both for our own pleasure and to bring joy to others.

8

Angels with a Purpose

Working consciously with angels gives us the opportunity to participate in creating more love and joy in the world. We can call on the angels who have been with humanity throughout history, or co-create more angels to help us with our lives in many ways. We can ask for their help for our family and friends, and they will happily join in when we initiate community projects, or when we set about building bridges and healing hurts. In this chapter I am going to make some suggestions for working with angels, in your private and family life, and in your wider community.

An Angel for Every Day of the Week

Traditionally, particular archangels have been assigned to the days of the week. However, traditions sometimes vary, and you may find variations in other books; for example, Gabriel is often associated with the moon, and therefore with Monday. But in my experience, the archangels listed below work well on these days:

Monday	Auriel	tenderness
Tuesday	Hanael	vitality
Wednesday	Gabriel	communication
Thursday	Zadkiel	abundance
Friday	Raphael	healing
Saturday	Samael	discipline
Sunday	Michael	leadership

You can find out more about these archangels in Chapter 10. If you have time after your morning meditation, you can call on the archangel for the day to assist you in your work and protect you as you go about your daily activities. You could also choose a particular day of the week to do something that you know would fit with the archangel's energy. For example, since Gabriel is the messenger, you might like to make important phone calls, and write and post letters, on Wednesdays. Hanael is assertive, so if you need to ask your boss for a rise, wait until Tuesday!

As well as working with the archangel for the day, you can also co-create an angel each morning especially to support your activities. In the morning, before you meditate, write down the things you have to do, the places you are going to, and anything you wish to achieve. Then visualise a little seed of light and ask it to grow into a strong angel to help you through the day. You can call this angel by the day of the week, for example 'My Monday angel'. You can do this every day during the first week, co-creating an angel for each day; then the following week, you can call on your personal Monday angel again. As most of us have routines and patterns to our lives, your daily angels will soon get to know what you need before you even ask. Week by week these angelic helpers will grow more in tune with you, and you with them.

Angels in the Healing Process

Many healers I talk to tell me they are aware of angelic presences during their healing sessions, and their patients often report feeling more than one pair of hands, or that they felt the warmth of invisible hands after the healer had finished working. Many healers work on a voluntary basis, or for a low cost, wishing to give loving support to others in need. The angels will naturally be attracted to such dedicated people, and healers hardly have to ask for their help.

The most beautiful angel to contact when healing is needed, whether emotional or physical, is the Archangel Raphael. The energy of this archangel is so soft, loving and harmonious that I usually refer to Raphael as 'she', though it is a shame that we do not assume that masculine energy can also be gentle and loving!

Raphael and Tobias

One of the most famous angel stories concerns Raphael and Tobias. It is told in the Apocrypha (a set of works written in biblical times but not included in the Protestant Bible). Although it is a little long I am including it in full, because it is a lovely story and demonstrates beautifully how angels work with divine economy: always seeking to solve many different problems by bringing the right people together. The story was a subject greatly loved by Renaissance painters.

On the very same day two people are praying to God. They both have life problems so great that they want to die. One of them is old Tobit, who has lost his eyesight and become very poor as a result; the other is Sarah, living many miles away, who has a man problem: every time she marries, a wicked demon called Asmodeus kills the husband 'before they had been with her as is customary for wives'. By the time the story starts Sarah has lost seven husbands in this way – no wonder she is desperate. At the very same moment the prayers of Tobit and Sarah are heard in the glorious presence of God, and Raphael is sent to heal them both.

The old man remembers that he has left some money in trust for over 20 years with a relative some distance away, and thinks it would be a good time to retrieve it. He wants his son Tobias to undertake this, but Tobias is reluctant; he doesn't even know the way. Tobit insists that Tobias go into town to find a guide; there Tobias meets a stranger who offers to guide him. Unbeknown to Tobias, the stranger is Raphael. Tobias takes his new guide to meet his old father, and they promise to pay Raphael a suitable fee for his trouble. Raphael says to Tobit: 'Take courage, the time is near for God to heal you.' Tobias's mother is very unsettled about her only son going off with a stranger, but the old man says, 'Do not fear … a good angel will accompany them.'

On the journey Tobias is washing his feet in the river, when a big fish tries to swallow his foot. His guide tells him to catch the fish and cut out its gall, heart and liver, which will make useful medicine. When they eventually reach their destination Tobias is introduced to Sarah, who turns out to be a distant relative, and his 'heart is drawn to her'. Raphael tells him he should marry Sarah – under Jewish law he had a special claim to marry into her family – and anyway she is 'sensible, brave and very beautiful'. Obviously Tobias is very nervous about the demon. But on Raphael's instructions, he burns the fish liver as incense on the bedroom fire. The smell repels the demon and Tobias and Sarah become happily married – Raphael is definitely the angel for weddings. This marriage is also financially beneficial, as Sarah has a large dowry (I think Raphael is quite good on the money side too!).

When Tobias goes home with his new wife, Raphael tells him to smear the fish gall on his father's eyes; this medicine enables them to peel away the cataracts and Tobit recovers his sight. They hold a wedding party and Tobias offers Raphael half the dowry he has brought home, as well as the payment already agreed. But Raphael tells him that it was he who brought their prayers before the Lord. 'I am one of the seven angels who stand ready and enter before the glory of the Lord ... when I was with you I was not acting on my own will, but by the will of God.'

Then, having achieved his task of weaving all the threads together, bringing healing and abundance to several people at once, Raphael ascends to heaven and they no longer see him. According to the story, Tobit was 62 when this happened, and went on to live to be 112 years old.

So, if you want to send healing to someone who needs help in a relationship, or who has a physical illness, Raphael is the archangel to call on. The best way to send angelic healing is to meditate and ask your guardian angel to create a link to Raphael for you, then ask the archangel to send healing to the other person, via their guardian angel. Tell them that you want to encourage healing, but recognise that you may not know what is best for the other person, and cannot manipulate the results. There may be a reason for the person's condition; they may have something to learn from it. And remember that sometimes people need to die in order to reconnect themselves with the spiritual world. We can never understand the whole story, but we can always ask for the best for others.

Asking for Healing

There is nothing to stop us asking for healing for ourselves.

Felicity has been dealing with cancer for a few years, and has had a couple of operations and chemotherapy. She had to give up her business but decided to train in holistic therapies and took my course to find out more about angels. She has to have a CAT scan every 6 weeks, which involves fasting for 24 hours and then drinking a horrible liquid for an hour and a quarter:

'When I finally go into the scanner the nurse has to insert a needle into my veins which pumps blue dye around my system. In five years they have never got the needle in first time, it normally takes five or six painful attempts. It is hard because my veins have shrunk since the chemotherapy.

'Last time, I started to pray to the angels beforehand. I asked Michael for strength and courage, and Raphael for healing and calm, and for days before the treatment I asked for the needle to be inserted the first time and prayed that my scan would be clear. I slept the night before using the angel meditation . . . I managed to drink the liquid without being sick, and to my amazement the needle went in first time. I asked Michael and Raphael to come with me to the scanner and I felt really calm.

'Two weeks later I visited the oncologist who said there was still no sign of the cancer. He was so pleased with my health that he said I do not have to have a scan or visit him for the next six months.'

Angels and Money

Money makes the world go round, says the song. Actually from an angelic perspective the world going round creates the money!

Money is a symbolic way of exchanging life energy. From ancient times until quite recently the currency of exchange was gold – this was a very significant symbol, since gold is the metal of the sun, which gives us energy. Nowadays money is symbolised by numbers on bank statements and we move it around using bits of plastic –

rarely do we handle large quantities of actual money. And another interesting thought is that the more zeros you have at the end of those numbers, the richer you are!

If you think of money as a game you are less likely to be ruled by it. This doesn't mean that you should be irresponsible with it, but a relaxed attitude will help it to flow freely. I find that visiting a foreign country and dealing with unfamiliar notes and coins can give you a new perspective. When teaching angel workshops in Norway I am paid in krone, which are approximately ten to the pound sterling, so instead of being paid, say, £30 I am paid K300. This means that I receive hundreds, instead of tens for the same work! And since the rate is not exact, I can't work out in my head how much it is in pounds, which gets in the way of my usual mental calculations. When forced in this way to let go of arithmetic I find that I receive exactly what I need. And this is how angels work with money. They don't care about a few zeros here or there. If you need £100 for your first guitar, it will come to you; if you need a million for something that is truly life enhancing for many people, and is part of your life purpose, that too will come to you.

Love and money are intimate bedfellows. If we feel unloved we feel unsupported and then we experience difficulties with money. If we feel we are not good enough, we project this on to our circumstances, so however much money we get it will not be good enough either. This is clear from the many cases we read in celebrity magazines of very wealthy people who suffer from addictions – their money isn't enough for them, and they are always looking for something more.

If you are feeling tested over money issues, the most important thing is to remind yourself constantly that you do have plenty – most people in the West have more than plenty – and acknowledge this daily, by counting your blessings, by saving money and by giving money.

In the story of Tobias, the Archangel Raphael reminds him that almsgiving is a key to salvation, and that giving alms is better than laying up gold. The word 'alms' comes from the Greek word for 'compassion', and generosity of spirit is expressed through giving, especially to those in need. Wherever humans focus their attention angels will gather, either the light and helpful ones or the testing ones. So we can be sure there are already plenty of money angels, and they will certainly bring more money to you if you are in the habit of giving plenty of it away. The scientists say that 'nature abhors a vacuum' – wherever there is a space something will fill it, and giving money away encourages more to flow towards you.

So do make a commitment to give 'alms'; even if you think you are broke there is always someone much poorer than you. When setting your budget, include giving, and ask the angels to help you choose an organisation or person to give to. You could set up a separate gift account. In the same way that a bank will allow you a second account called 'household account', you can ask them to call it 'gift account' – most banks are very amenable, so you may even be able to have 'angel account' on your cheques. Make it an opportunity to test the co-creation of angels. Use the co-creating visualisation described on page 125 to create a new angel to watch over this account. Regularly put 10 per cent of your earnings into it and then write cheques from it to give to others. Although many charities ask us to make regular payments by direct debit, which enables them to claim tax benefits, it is also really delightful to be able to give spontaneously; having money in a special giving account allows you to make a donation on the spur of the moment.

At the same time as creating an angel account for giving, create a savings account for treats for yourself, such as that really amazing holiday or journey that you have always dreamed about, and another for a special purchase which will improve your life – one of my accounts is presently allocated to a laptop. Visualise an angel who is helping you accumulate the money in these accounts. You can co-create lots of money angels to help you increase your income so that you can give more to others, as well as creating the financial freedom to follow your real life path. I find accounts that have passbooks much more fun than Internet accounts or those using plastic cards.

The angel of wealth and abundance is the Archangel Zadkiel (see page 157). If you are starting a new venture, such as setting up your own business or selling and buying a house, ask Zadkiel to support you. When you have done some work with Zadkiel from Chapter 10, you could create your own image of this exuberant and generous character and keep it with your account books.

Angels to Comfort the Dying

Traditionally, angels are associated with the dying – think of the number we see in churchyards. And that's not surprising, for they are always present to help people on their way to the next life.

The Comforter

At my brother's fiftieth birthday party, one of his friends, a Norwegian woman called Trude, told me a remarkable story.

When Trude's aunt was dying in hospital, the old lady told her daughter (Trude's cousin) that she had been visited by an angel. The daughter was very surprised, because her mother had never had any spiritual interests at all. The dying lady was quite excited and said the angel had given her his name – Azrael. Back home, the daughter researched the name of this angel and discovered that Azrael is the Angel of Death. A few days later the old lady died.

People who work in hospitals are very aware that dying people receive deathbed visitors from other realms. Sometimes these are 'beings of light', sometimes they are the spirits of relatives. A Methodist minister told me that when she visits the dying, the nurses will often say things like: 'Old Tom won't be here much longer, his mum came last night.' Deathbed visions and near-death experiences confirm that a dying person gets help, both from relatives who have already died and from light beings of extraordinary compassion who help the person to review their life and understand their connection to all beings. These experiences have been recorded throughout the ages and have helped humans to understand that this life is not the only one.

It seems that each person leaves at exactly the right time. Several traditional stories tell of people who have heard that the Angel of Death is looking for them; when they try to escape to another city, the angel meets them there. When it is time to go, the appointment cannot be changed. A few years ago someone very close to me knew that he was 'over the limit' and, in the interest of his personal safety, took a taxi home instead of using his car. After he got out of the taxi he walked up a very familiar path to his flat, but tripped and fell a few feet down a rocky slope. The damage to his ribs and head proved fatal; his safety precautions had been to no avail.

Conversely, you cannot leave before the right time either, even if you would like to. One old lady was in hospital with a broken leg. She was 90, had had a full life, and was quite ready to go. One night, she was visited by three 'tall people' who stood by her hospital bed looking at her; then they shook their heads, as though to say, 'No, it's not time yet.' She knew that it wasn't a dream because a moment later a nurse came by, and the old lady asked, 'Have my visitors gone?' She lived for five more years.

If we want to support and help someone who is dying, we can provide comfort just by sitting quietly and saying prayers, or reading them poetry and inspirational words. We can also bring them beautiful music to listen to. The great composers wrote requiem music to assist the soul on its journey. I would certainly love to hear Mozart's Requiem when I am on my deathbed.

When my best female friend, Rachael, was dying with cancer I stayed in the hospital for the last week of her life, most of the day and night, massaging her feet, and helping her create the programme for her funeral – or, as she called it, her recycling event! We had worked together with the angels, so we could talk freely about the support she would receive from them as she moved into the next stage of her soul's process. I fully expect to meet her again, perhaps in a future life.

Sometimes a dying person needs permission to leave from the people who have been dependent on them. My cousin was nursing her elderly mother at home and one day she suddenly found herself saying, 'It's all right Mum, you can go now.' Almost immediately she witnessed her mother passing peacefully away. It was if she had been hanging on, as a good mother who did not want to desert her children.

Some of the taboos that surround death are gradually being lifted but there are some people who might not be happy if you started to talk to them about the angels who help the dying. You can still help them, without mentioning angels. One way would be to place a photograph of the person in your sacred space when you meditate. Ask your guardian angel to help you create a bridge to the person and send them the love and healing that they need. Do not try to interfere with their process. It is not useful to wish or pray for someone to live, when they need to go, or to pray for them to have an easy death when they have the resources to continue. Ask Raphael to help in whatever way is appropriate.

The Archangel Gabriel can also help during the death process since he creates the bridge between the celestial and the natural worlds. Because Gabriel can act as a guide for the soul, it would be useful to call on him at the point when the person has actually died. In the Tibetan tradition the lamas pray for the dead for 49 days, which is the time the soul takes to go through the *bardo*, the after-death plane. Forty-nine is the square of the sacred number seven and I believe that seven archangels will assist you through different levels as you leave (see Chapter 10). I haven't been there myself, of course, but this is in accordance with ancient traditions, and reports by the mystics who have journeyed through the seven heavens and have returned to their bodies. We cannot know whether it will take literally 49 days of our time to move through the afterlife process, because time becomes very different for the soul after leaving the body. However, you could keep a loved one in your meditations for several weeks after they have died, calling on the angels to help them adjust to a new way of being.

You do not need to call on Azrael. The Angel of Death will be present automatically at the due time. He can appear in many guises – and he is not to be feared.

Angels of Places and Nations

In the Book of Daniel the Archangel Michael appears to Daniel in a wonderful vision – Daniel is so overwhelmed that he falls to the ground in a trance. Michael tells him he is the princely protector of Israel and that he will support the Israelites against the princes of other nations like Persia and Greece. Now this does sound like a case of 'my angel is stronger than yours!', which is a rather outmoded way for humans to think about divine energy. But there is a long tradition associating angels with places and nations.

Some places that are associated with prayer and spirituality possess angels who were nurtured in centuries past by saints and hermits. These might be ancient religious sites, such as stone circles, or ancient chapels or temples. Britain is full of these old sites – not for nothing were these islands called the Blessed Isles in ancient times – and if we visit them we can tune into their energy and connect with their angels.

Before the Reformation, the many wonderful churches, abbeys and cathedrals in Britain would vibrate with 'perpetual choirs' created by the monks and nuns chanting around the clock. This energy created an etheric sanctuary, encouraging great celestial beings to protect the landscape and the people who lived here. This energy has not entirely faded, but it does need to be kept alive, not only in Britain but also in all countries. Research your own geographical area to find a place where spiritual activities have taken place and go there regularly to meditate yourself; you can engage with reawakening an angel who has been 'resting' and develop a relationship with it.

Angels don't only work in beautiful places: although it is easier for us to be open to them when the environment is calm and unthreatening, we can also connect to them in difficult times and in places which seem totally empty of spirituality. Human intentions and thoughts contribute to the energy of a place and we can actively participate in clearing negative places – for example, by inviting friends to create an 'angel circle', which meets regularly to meditate and send angelic energy to places which need help.

Each nation has an archangel, and the archangels are supported by

Sandalphon, the archangel of our planet and the human race. The names of these national archangels have not been recorded anywhere, but many people believe Michael is the archangel for England; he does have similarities with the patron saint of England, St George who, like Michael, is depicted slaying a dragon. In the past England was seen as a significant world leader, so people probably felt that Michael, 'commander in chief' of all angels, was a suitable archangel for the English nation.

Each national archangel takes the various threads which make up a nation: the characteristics of the people, and the karma they create – through both their positive contributions and their mistakes – and weaves them into a splendid, many-hued tapestry as the nation unfolds its identity and its destiny. All nations grow and change over time, adjusting perhaps to immigration or to climate changes, and the national archangel will grow and change as well.

Whatever your nationality, you will be able to tune into the archangel for your nation. Even very small countries will have an overlighting archangel. In his now out-of-print book *The Coming of the Angels*, the theosophist Geoffrey Hodson describes a vision he had in the Isle of Man, where he saw a majestic, Herculean figure looking down on the island from the top of Snaefell; he also received an impression of the name 'Manaan'. It is quite clear, from the work of many people involved in landscape energy research, that we will most easily make contact with our national archangels in high places of great beauty and serenity.

In my own work, I have become aware that the British Isles also have a number of regional angels working with distinctive groups, such as the Cornish people, the Avalonians, who live in Somerset and Avon, the Northumbrians, and so on. My impression is that there are 12 of these angels in Britain, and each is centred on a sacred place of some kind, either a religious building or a natural beauty spot. I would be very interested to hear from people who want to work in their area, to encourage the awakening and energising of the regional angels. I am quite sure that regional angels will also be found in all other countries with distinctive regional characteristics.

The millions of human personalities who make up a nation

participate, mostly unconsciously, in the way their archangel develops as their national over-soul. But if a nation takes up an aggressive position towards other nations, this may enable a dark entity to overrule the highest possibility of the national culture, which can lead its people, and many others, into war, with terrible consequences. Although many of us nowadays do not participate in conventional church prayers, I believe it is essential that we all meditate on world peace and encourage our national angels to overlight our leaders.

At times of great national concern, when there is a disaster, or an impending conflict, we can gather together in groups, either creating a sacred space for ourselves or using local facilities, such as a meeting house, church, mosque, temple or synagogue. At such times, meditate quietly together and inwardly call on the archangel of your nation to make his presence felt (you may receive an impression of his name at this time). Then ask the archangel to work with the leaders of your nation, or if appropriate with the national services, such as the fire brigade or the police, who may be under great stress while dealing with a disaster. Ask for protection and comfort, but do not think of your national archangel as being in conflict with the archangel of another nation – celestial beings do not support strife and war; they are looking for ways to encourage humans to settle their differences peacefully.

9

The Archangels of the Zodiac

In the last chapter I described how archangels overlight nations and places. There are also many archangels overlighting different kinds of groups – people who come together for various purposes; these are the soul group archangels. Whenever people are gathered together in a group they will help to co-create an angel that will grow from their energy. This applies to families, playgroups, schools and colleges, hospitals, religious groups and so on.

In addition to these, there are many, many archangels who have been in place from the beginning of time, and who overlight different aspects of creation. The most important for human beings are the archangels who are the guardians of the signs of the zodiac.

Finding Your Solar Archangel

In Chapter 6 I suggested a visualisation to help you connect with your solar archangel, who overlights your sign of the zodiac. In this chapter I will be giving you all the information you need to work with this archangel in other ways.

Most people know their zodiac sun sign, but if you are not sure of yours, you will find the dates for each sign shown on the archangel pages in this chapter. If you were born on the cusp (the very day when the sign changes) it could be useful to ask an astrologer or use an Internet site to double check. If you are a 'cusp' person it would be useful to find out the time of day you were born. You might think you are an Aries person, but find that you were born at the end of the day, when the sun had just entered the sign of Taurus. Another way to decide which archangel is correct for you is to read the information for both archangels (Aries and Taurus) and see which one resonates with you.

The Importance of the Zodiac Archangels

For human beings, the sun is the most powerful energy-giving body in the heavens. We depend on it for our life force and it symbolises our passion and enthusiasm for life. The sun represents our inner kingship, our heart and our sovereign self. If we want to take charge of our own destiny and create a life that is meaningful and fulfilling, then we need to be in touch with our inner ruler.

As the sun appears to move around the earth it passes through 12 sections of the sky. Each section is named after a constellation, such as Aries the Ram, Taurus the Bull and so on. (Because most of the constellations are named after animals, with one or two humans as well, these 12 are called the signs of the zodiac – the Greek word *zoion* means 'life form'). The sun consists of pure energy, but as it moves through the signs it takes on different qualities. Think of placing a series of different-coloured filters in front of a light – with each filter the same light creates a different effect. The light of spiritual energy is similarly uncoloured and simple, but we experience it through a creative prism that breaks it into many colours and qualities. And one way of thinking about the archangels and other celestial beings is as fragments of divine light, which help to create the variety and many-layered possibilities that we experience in life. The high priests of ancient religions understood the importance of these different energies; the Jewish priests, for instance, included in their regalia a gold breastplate with 12 different precious stones set into it, representing the power of the 12 variations of divine light.

Each zodiac sign has an archangel overlighting it. Individually, these archangels represent different facets of divine energy; collectively they maintain an invisible architecture that sustains creation. In a great cathedral each pillar must be strong in its own right, but none can hold up the roof alone. Every one of us is a member of one of 12 soul groups, working – whether we know this consciously or not – towards the highest evolutionary possibility for the human race. When you work individually with your solar archangel you are able to strengthen your own highest potential, and at the same time contribute to the evolution of humanity as a whole.

Each zodiac sign is governed by a planet, and the planets are also overlit by archangels, so when you work with your solar archangel you will also be supported by a second archangel – the one who overlights the planet that governs your sun sign. I will be describing the planetary archangels, and how you can work with them, in Chapter 10.

I think you will find it useful and inspiring to read the pages for all the zodiac archangels, not just your own. Each archangel represents a configuration of different qualities: some have a yang, masculine energy; some have yin, feminine energy. As with the zodiac signs, there are three archangels for each of the four elements, fire, air, water and earth – so they each connect us with one of the four worlds. And these three have different qualities: cardinal, which has an initiating, forward-moving energy; fixed, which has a determined, getting-on-with-the-job energy; and mutable, which has a moving or sharing energy. As you read through the descriptions of the archangels in the rest of this chapter, you will come to realise that each has a part to play in the whole picture of creation.

How to Work with Your Solar Archangel

Once you have met your solar archangel, you will be able to maintain a relationship with him by visiting the circular room, which you discovered in the exercise in Chapter 6. Just as you can consult your guardian angel on a day-to-day basis, you can also call in your solar archangel, especially if there are serious, life-changing decisions to be made. You can create a 'board meeting' with both of them for important consultations.

One very important date you can make with your solar archangel is your own birthday. As part of your annual celebration, allow time for a special meditation. Before you begin, write down any ideas or questions you have about your life at present and the year ahead. In the same way that people write down their New Year's resolutions, you can make decisions for change and any new possibilities that you want to bring into your life. Use the session to ask both your guardian angel and your solar archangel for their advice and support for your plans and goals for the year ahead.

An Archangel Soul Group

Your solar archangel of course watches over and supports all the many other people born under the same sign of the zodiac as yourself. If you know other people who share your sun sign and are interested in spiritual development, you could suggest that you all meet, say, once a month, and meditate together, asking the solar archangel for the group to be present and to bring through any wisdom or insights that are needed. Wherever several people gather together with a single focus, great things can be manifested.

SARAQUAEL – I am

Archangel for the sign of
ARIES 21 March–20 April

ELEMENT Fire (Yang)
PLANETARY ARCHANGEL Hanael – Mars
SACRED STONES Diamond, Bloodstone
SACRED GIFT A Diamond Crown
QUALITY Cardinal

KEYWORDS Hope, Action
COLOUR Red
METAL Iron
MANIFESTATION Enterprise, Energy

Saraquael is the first archangel of the zodiac circuit; he is also a seraph and his energy comes in with fiery, initiatory energy. Saraquael's fire energy is cleansing; he is able to burn up the past and clear the way for new things to happen.

If you were born with Archangel Saraquael overlighting your life, you will have first-hand knowledge of the driving force of his energy field. He asks you to shatter old ideas and bring in the new, to create far-reaching new concepts and inspire others to follow your beacon. He is a visionary, bringing ancient knowledge and purity of thought.

In order to live up to this highly charged archangel you will have to be prepared to take risks, dare to experiment with life and not take the safe path. When you commit to working with Saraquael you will glow with a charisma that attracts other people to work with you, or even to follow you, and this requires that you become aware of your responsibility to others. You will be a leader. Be clear what your goal is and the creative power of the Divine will be at your disposal.

INVOCATION TO SARAQUAEL

Archangel Saraquael, it is my birthright to work with you and I am willing to be a channel for the highest possibility we can create together. Fill me with hope, courage and energy. Crown me with inspiration and charge me with divine purpose. Connect me with the ancient wisdom and keep my thoughts and motivation pure so that I may use my divine gifts for the greater good.

ASHMODIEL – I become

Archangel for the sign of
TAURUS 21 April–20 May

ELEMENT Earth (Yin)
PLANETARY ARCHANGEL Sandalphon
– Earth
SACRED STONES Emerald, Moss Agate
SACRED GIFT An Emerald Necklace
QUALITY Fixed

KEYWORDS Peace, Stability
COLOUR Green
METAL Copper
MANIFESTATION Steadfastness,
Stewardship

Ashmodiel brings the visions of the Divine into manifestation. She seeks to bring the invisible glory into physical reality; she has a determination to create heaven on earth, because she knows that visions have no value until they are made real.

Ashmodiel carries a fixed, earth energy and is connected to the fourth world, the realm of the devas and nature spirits. Her generosity allows nature to unfold in all manner of ways – as mountains and valleys, lakes and deserts, volcanoes and glaciers. She can be gentle but she can be stern. There is a practical, mothering energy about Ashmodiel and you can feel her presence when the trees are full of blossom, and the green glory of spring flows over the landscape.

Ashmodiel is serene and has a calm, quiet power. She is a builder and will help you carry through your plans, giving you complete conviction that you will achieve your goals. When you work with Ashmodiel you become a creator, able to make your mark in the physical world. You have the capacity to attract great wealth and abundance, but you understand that you are a steward, not an owner, of the wealth you create.

INVOCATION TO ASHMODIEL

Archangel Ashmodiel, it is my birthright to work with you and I am willing to be a channel for the highest possibility we can create together. Fill me with determination, serenity and calm power. Help me to work towards a goal that is both useful and beautiful. Bring me the gifts I need in order to manifest a vision for the benefit of all and help me to be a wise protector and steward of planet earth.

AMBRIEL – I circulate

Archangel for the sign of
GEMINI 21 May–20 June

ELEMENT Air (Yang)
PLANETARY ARCHANGEL Gabriel –
  Mercury
SACRED STONES Beryl, Aquamarine
SACRED GIFT A Horn of Agate

QUALITY Mutable
KEYWORDS Variety, Joy
COLOUR Yellow
METAL Quicksilver
MANIFESTATION Invention, Change

Ambriel has a light energy; he moves quickly from place to place, whispering in trees, skimming clouds, then dipping and curving into the depths of the earth. He is most comfortable in the second world of air, but he can move easily from one world to the next, from light to dark and back again. He brings new thoughts and new ideas, always seeking inventive ways to solve problems and create exciting possibilities. Do not expect Ambriel always to be the same: he is a shape-shifting archangel, able to take on different guises.

Ambriel will bring you messages from the Divine and he asks you to work with integrity and always be committed to the truth. When you work with Ambriel you will be given the facility to communicate through words, or through music and poetry, dance or painting. If you commit yourself to being a clear channel for divine communication you may also become an oracle or a wise prophet. People will be enchanted by the divine gifts you have to offer and you will be able to transform the lives of many when you use your gifts for the benefit of all.

INVOCATION TO AMBRIEL

Archangel Ambriel, it is my birthright to work with you and I am willing to be a channel for the highest possibility we can create together. Open my mind to the music of the spheres, to the sacred words of the Divine, to the visions of the stars. Allow me to communicate with wisdom and integrity so that every word I speak is for the greater glory of the divine purpose.

CAEL – I create

Archangel for the sign of
CANCER 21 June–21 July

ELEMENT Water (Yin)
PLANETARY ARCHANGEL Auriel – the Moon
SACRED STONES Pearl, Selenite
SACRED GIFT Mother-of-pearl Breastplate

QUALITY Cardinal
KEYWORDS Patience, Sympathy
COLOUR Sea-blue
METAL Silver
MANIFESTATION Imagination, Flexibility

Cael has a nurturing, feminine energy. She is able to give boundless loving care from a deep source, because she is connected to the wellspring of divine love. Her element is water so she connects you easily to the third world. She is an initiator; like a cascading waterfall or a babbling brook she brings fresh joy and delight, baptising all she touches with the dewdrops and gentle rain from heaven. She treads lightly on the earth, creating a shimmer of gentle beauty wherever she goes. You will feel her presence on a moonlit night, and the fairies are under her care.

She welcomes those in need of healing and calls small children to her knee. She is a wise teacher and a prophetess, who offers an oracle to those who will listen to her intuitive wisdom, drawn from the silent depths of the cosmic ocean.

Cael asks you to become a priest or priestess of the feminine power, to protect and nourish the vulnerable, to offer comfort to the needy. When you work with Cael you have easy access to a boundless ocean of loving kindness and she asks you to offer this to the world without condition.

INVOCATION TO CAEL

Archangel Cael, it is my birthright to work with you and I am willing to be a channel for the highest possibility we can create together. Fill my heart with the wisdom of boundless love. Fill my soul with your radiance and beauty. Heal my own hurts, so that I may heal others. Feed me with divine knowledge so that I can teach others the way of loving kindness. Strengthen my commitment to love unconditionally.

ZERACHIEL – I rule

Archangel for the sign of
LEO 22 July–21 Aug

ELEMENT Fire (Yang)
PLANETARY ARCHANGEL Michael
  – the Sun
SACRED STONES Ruby, Cat's Eye
SACRED GIFT A Golden Shield

QUALITY Fixed
KEYWORDS Glory, Faith
COLOUR Orange
METAL Gold
MANIFESTATION Radiance, Understanding

Zerachiel is like a king, a shining ruler in a golden chariot. His element is fire and he works with the seraphim. His energy is fixed, and he has the will and the determination to act as a centre point, a pivot around which many other celestial beings will hover. He brings great enthusiasm and a vitality that illuminates the lives of all who meet him or get to know him. Even though he seems overwhelming in his glory, his spirit is generous and warm, and his radiance brings hope and glory into the world on days when everything seems grey.

Like a benevolent father, Zerachiel enfolds you within a protective cloak of certainty and new courage. His tenacity will encourage you to go forward even when you feel lost. When you work with Zerachiel you discover that the abundance of the Divine is unlimited, and as long as you keep giving, you will keep receiving. He asks you to take charge, to demonstrate your kingship, but also to develop nobility and generosity of spirit, and to keep your heart wide open to all comers, always looking for the divine spark in everyone you meet.

INVOCATION TO ZERACHIEL

Archangel Zerachiel, it is my birthright to work with you and I am willing to be a channel for the highest possibility we can create together. Let my heart beat with a new courage, so that I can illuminate the world with divine energy. I am committed to act in the world with nobility and dignity, bringing hope and joy to all those I meet. Surround me with your radiant glory and remind me of your infinite abundance.

VAEL – I provide

Archangel for the sign of
Virgo 22 August–21 September

ELEMENT Earth (Yin)
PLANETARY ARCHANGEL The Shekinah – Charon (the Moon of Pluto)
SACRED STONES Pink Jasper, Hyacinth
SACRED GIFT A Girdle Set with Jasper

QUALITY Mutable
KEYWORDS Purity, Service
COLOUR White
METAL Platinum
MANIFESTATION Discrimination, Grace

Vael is both the mysterious Lady of the Earth, mistress of devas and nature spirits, and the invisible Queen of the Heavens. Her feet move silently in our world, but she is crowned by shining stars. Her energy changes through the seasons: quiet under the snow in winter, veiled with white blossoms in spring, abundant with produce in summer. In the autumn we see the signs of her earthly work in baskets of ripe fruit, sheaves of corn, and nature's cornucopia of abundance. But she also works within the soul, summoning you to clear the way for divine beauty and grace.

When you are called to work with Vael, there will be no trumpets or earthquakes in your soul, just the quiet insistence that you must commit to clarity and to a path of discrimination. Vael asks you to serve the Divine Spirit by healing the land, working with nature spirits, providing for the poor and needy, and choosing only the highest possibilities for yourself and those in your care. Vael will provide exactly what is needed, to the highest standard; do not accept anything in your life that is not worthy of the Divine Spirit.

INVOCATION TO VAEL

Archangel Vael, it is my birthright to work with you and I am willing to be a channel for the highest possibility we can create together. Bring your quiet certainty into my soul and help me to discriminate without condemning. Allow me to serve the highest purpose of divine love. Connect me with your endless bounty of love and life and let me be an overflowing chalice of divine joy.

ZURIEL – I soothe

Archangel for the sign of
LIBRA 22 September–22 October

ELEMENT Air (Yang)
PLANETARY ARCHANGEL Raphael
  – Venus
SACRED STONES Opal, Amethyst
SACRED GIFT An Opal Scabbard

QUALITY Cardinal
KEYWORDS Beauty, Harmony
COLOUR Lilac
METAL Copper
MANIFESTATION Balance, Equilibrium

Zuriel is connected to the second world of air and he initiates truth and wisdom wherever there is discord. He balances all the oppositions, of light and dark, of life and death. He understands both sides of every divine coin, and weighs hearts and souls and minds on silver scales. His energy is like the calm splendour of an evening sunset when the sky is bathed in lilac and the clouds blush with a soft rose pink. He is active, but does not act until all the choices have been considered and weighed in the balance.

Zuriel will help you see all things as equal and you will understand the nature of divine harmony, beauty and grace. When you know the world through this archangel you will see the inner perfection of all creation and you will gain direct knowledge of the divine laws, which govern our lives.

Zuriel asks you to become a champion for the needy; to bring peace where there is strife; to speak only words of wisdom and divine law, righteousness and truth; to take light into dark places, to serve justice and freedom for all creatures.

INVOCATION TO ZURIEL

Archangel Zuriel, it is my birthright to work with you and I am willing to be a channel for the highest possibility we can create together. Let me walk the path of truth, justice and freedom. Inspire me to speak the words of divine law, seeking only balance and harmony and never retribution. Help me to stay centred and calm and to bring stillness and peace wherever I go.

BARUEL – I heal

Archangel for the sign of
SCORPIO 23 October–21 November

ELEMENT Water (Yin)
PLANETARY ARCHANGEL Metatron
  – Pluto
SACRED STONES Topaz, Malachite
SACRED GIFT A Dagger Jewelled
  with Topaz

QUALITY Fixed
KEYWORDS Justice, Power
COLOUR Black
METAL Steel
MANIFESTATION Determination,
  Vigilance

Baruel works in the world of water, and allows you to explore the depths of consciousness. Her energy is like a coiled spring, containing the power for dramatic transformation. She is mysterious and moves silently and secretly, with a certain knowledge of the inner, metaphysical worlds from which creation unfolds. Because she is so connected to the dark mysteries she is able to heal physical and emotional hurts. She understands the depths of the human soul and brings solace to those in pain. She has a direct perception of the karmic processes at work in the destinies of human beings, and brings gifts of clairvoyance and intuition.

When you work with Baruel you need to be disciplined, vigilant and resilient. She asks you to take up your power, but temper it with wisdom and compassion. You can work with extraordinary psychic or paranormal powers, but this means that you have to be exceptionally conscientious and totally aware of your responsibility for the results. Self-mastery is the path of those who are committed to working with Baruel. Do not be afraid to act, the universe supports your commitment to bring renewal out of darkness.

INVOCATION TO BARUEL

Archangel Baruel, it is my birthright to work with you and I am willing to be a channel for the highest possibility we can create together. Watch over me as I learn how to use power wisely. Allow me to understand the deep secrets of the universe and guide me to use my inner knowledge for the benefit of others. Open my heart to divine compassion so that my energy is directed where it most needed.

ADNACHIEL – I encourage

Archangel for the sign of
SAGITTARIUS 22 November–20 December

ELEMENT Fire (Yang)
PLANETARY ARCHANGEL Zadkiel –
Jupiter
SACRED STONES Turquoise, Lapis Lazuli
SACRED GIFT A Bow Studded with
Lapis Lazuli

QUALITY Mutable
KEYWORDS Wisdom, Law, Freedom
COLOUR Purple
METAL Tin
MANIFESTATION Creativity, Justice

Adnachiel is a fiery archangel, calling you to far visions and distant lands. He brings inspiration into the hearts and souls of human beings, summoning them to seek divine wisdom. Adnachiel is majestic and grand, and the mighty choir of the seraphim from the first world surround him.

You are being summoned to be a wise counsellor, to encourage others to see the Divine in the universe, to declare the glory of all creation. With Adnachiel by your side you can go on inner journeys to meet wise teachers who will guide you, or celestial beings, those who watch over our own planet and others from distant galaxies. You will be inspired to prophesy and to teach, to learn from spiritual traditions and then to bring new insights. Divine wisdom, freedom and generosity of spirit are the gifts of Adnachiel.

Your insights will allow you to understand the souls of other beings and you will feel called to work as a priest, a guide or a counsellor, and this means you must be tolerant and honest. Strive for the highest possibilities and your visions will bring joy and hope to many.

INVOCATION TO ADNACHIEL

Archangel Adnachiel, it is my birthright to work with you and I am willing to be a channel for the highest possibility we can create together. Take me on a journey through the celestial worlds, so I can meet the guides and teachers that will help me on my path. Give me insight and wisdom, fill me with divine energy so that I can live with enthusiasm and bring messages of hope and freedom to all those I meet.

ORPHIEL – I order

Archangel for the sign of
CAPRICORN 21 December–19 January

ELEMENT Earth (Yin)
PLANETARY ARCHANGEL Samael
  – Saturn
SACRED STONES Jet, Tourmaline
SACRED GIFT An Antique
  Casket

QUALITY Cardinal
KEYWORDS Reverence, Excellence
COLOUR Indigo
METAL Lead
MANIFESTATION Concentration,
  Worldly Power

Orphiel works in the fourth world, of earthly manifestation. She helps to create structures and enables you to set goals and strive towards them. Orphiel has a cool energy, and is determined and powerful. She may seem like a snow queen on a high mountain, but her heart is not made of ice; she is committed and totally dedicated to creating a concrete reality based on divine wisdom. Do not underestimate her passion; she has a mother's tenacity and her intentions are based on the timeless laws.

Working with Orphiel puts you in touch with the patterns of creative energy, which underpin the world. Just as every snowflake has a unique crystalline structure, so each human endeavour is based on invisible patterns that unfold through time until we see the final result. Orphiel allows you to understand those underlying structures and the natural laws of the universe. This knowledge allows you to appreciate spiritual traditions and to accept divine authority.

Orphiel asks you to be cautious and prudent; to use worldly power for heavenly purposes; to be focussed, discreet and determined. Speak only the highest truth and only deliver judgement when you have understood the wisdom of natural law.

INVOCATION TO ORPHIEL

Archangel Orphiel, it is my birthright to work with you and I am willing to be a channel for the highest possibility we can create together. Help me to be cautious but not cold; prudent but not closed. Teach me the hidden laws of universal wisdom and direct me to use this knowledge with discrimination. I am committed to discipline, which brings freedom, and to using my will with kindness.

CAMBIEL – I empower

Archangel for the sign of
AQUARIUS 20 January–18 February

ELEMENT Air (Yang)
PLANETARY ARCHANGEL Raziel –
  Uranus
SACRED STONES Sapphire, Blue Topaz
SACRED GIFT A Sapphire Ring

QUALITY Fixed
KEYWORDS Truth, Investigation
COLOUR Electric Blue
METAL Aluminium
MANIFESTATION Curiosity, Revolution

Cambiel is an archangel from the realms of air. He belongs in the stillness of the night air, or high above the clouds. He soars like an eagle, watching the grandeur of life from a place of calm and equanimity. He sees all things in creation from a great height and brings you an understanding of the equality of all God's creatures. He sees above, below and beyond, and showers inspiration, grace and blessings without favour.

When you are called to work with Cambiel you will be privileged to understand the unity of divine creation, and will understand that the divine laws apply to all creation. You will be a truth seeker or a scientist, and will be guided by traditional values but also prepared to overturn outmoded rules and regulations. Liberty, equality and justice are your motivations.

Cambiel tells you that divine power is the key to liberation and that this must be used wisely, or the consequences will be severe. He asks you to take up freedom and responsibility, to give generously, and to champion the foolish and the needy. You are able to open doors for others to see the light.

INVOCATION TO CAMBIEL

Archangel Cambiel, it is my birthright to work with you and I am willing to be a channel for the highest possibility we can create together. Take me to the airy heights, so that I can see the equality of all God's creatures. Fill me with divine grace, so that I can bring inspiration and blessings to all those I meet. Give me wisdom and insight to work for change and spiritual freedom.

BARAKIEL – I love

Archangel for the sign of
PISCES 19 February–20 March

ELEMENT Water (Yin)
PLANETARY ARCHANGEL Zaphkiel –
  Neptune
SACRED STONES Rose Quartz,
  Moonstone
SACRED GIFT Seashell Slippers

QUALITY Mutable
KEYWORDS Love, Unity
COLOUR Rose Pink
METAL Platinum
MANIFESTATION Insight,
  Clairvoyance

Barakiel brings wisdom from the ocean of the collective consciousness of humanity, which is connected to the source of divine compassion. Barakiel is a loving mother, who emerges from the world of water and moves with gentle tides across your soul. She shimmers like a mermaid and brings wordless knowledge from beyond the edge of time. She is contained in the heart of the Divine, where she breathes softly, bringing love towards her then releasing it to us. Her love unfolds in our hearts, like a rose or a lotus unfolding its soft petals.

When you work with Barakiel you will understand the nature of boundless love. You will realise the closeness of your own soul to heaven. You will know that your own soul is timeless and immortal, that there is no death, only the endless and infinite life-giving power of God.

Barakiel asks you to surrender yourself to divine love. She asks you to give ceaselessly, so that she can fill you, over and over again with her own unconditional love. With Barakiel there is no fear for the future, no regret for the past, she heals hurts and washes away old wounds.

INVOCATION TO BARAKIEL

Archangel Barakiel, it is my birthright to work with you and I am willing to be a channel for the highest possibility we can create together. Fill me with divine love, so that I may give unconditionally. Bring me dreams and visions, so that I may inspire others to experience your beauty and loving tenderness. Breathe with me, fill me with divine light, so that I can bring divine wisdom into the world.

10

The Archangels of the Tree of Life

The 12 best-known archangels belong to the Tree of Life, which is an ancient symbol for the cycle of life, death and resurrection. In nature, the tree grows from a seedling into a sapling, then into a mature tree, which may live for many centuries. The tree grows leaves, flowers and fruit, which fall away in the autumn, becoming rich compost at the foot of the tree, which feeds new growth the following spring. The tree, as a symbol for the ever-flowing energy of spirit, can be found in many spiritual traditions, but the most beautiful version can be found in the Jewish mystical teaching called the Kabbalah.

The medieval Kabbalists created a stylised diagram of the Tree of Life, which is shown in the illustration on the next page. The Kabbalistic Tree of Life illustrates the way divine energy flows through all aspects of creation, from tiny cells to the great galaxies. The energy emerges from a deep and mysterious source that is beyond our understanding, and creates a 'crown' at the top of the Tree, which supplies the spiritual power for growth and development. From this crown, in which active and passive (yang and yin) are held in balance, the energy flows through a series of channels and containers until it is grounded at the foot of the Tree – the 'kingdom'. The containers, shown as circles in the illustration, are called '*sefiroth*' (the singular word is '*sefira*') and they represent the different qualities

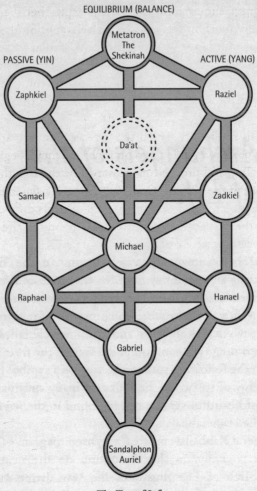

EQUILIBRIUM (BALANCE)

Metatron
The
Shekinah

PASSIVE (YIN)

Zaphkiel

ACTIVE (YANG)

Raziel

Da'at

Samael

Zadkiel

Michael

Raphael

Hanael

Gabriel

Sandalphon
Auriel

The Tree of Life

of the Divine. The top *sefira*, the crown, is connected to the Divine Source and through it pours the *shefa*, which means 'everflow', and is equivalent to *prana*, or the life force. The *shefa* pours into the channels, which gradually fill each container – rather like water flowing downwards and filling up a series of reservoirs.

The diagram shows how the energy shifts between two outer pillars, passive (yin) on the left and active (yang) on the right, and a central pillar of balance or equilibrium. (A similar system is seen in yoga, where the chakras vibrate along the central channel created by the human spine, and two channels weave around the body, the *ida*: the lunar, or yin channel, and the *pingala*: the solar or yang channel.)

The Jewish mystics regarded the Tree of Life as a spiritual map, which they used as a guide to go on inner journeys, beginning at the foot of the Tree and proceeding upwards. At the top, they hoped to get a glimpse of the glory of God. Visiting each *sefira* in turn involves coming to a direct understanding of each of God's different qualities. Sometimes the *sefiroth* are called 'the divine hands' or 'the divine faces', while the Tree is thought of as the body of God.

There are ten *sefiroth*, also known as 'gates of light', on the Tree of Life, plus one mysterious 'non-*sefira*', called Da'at, which means knowledge (marked on the diagram as a circle with broken lines). We can think of Da'at as the veil between the worlds; the *sefiroth* above it are so mysterious and powerful that the mystical seeker had to be very holy in order to move beyond it and approach the three heavenly *sefiroth* that make up the 'divine throne'.

Each *sefira* is watched over by an archangel, with two archangels each at the top and the foot of the Tree, making 12 in all. These 12 archangels overlight the heavenly bodies of our solar system and, along with the zodiac archangels, are some of the most powerful celestial beings you are likely to meet. They include the four archangels of the directions – Michael, Gabriel, Raphael and Auriel – and others whose names you may have come across, such as Metatron, Zadkiel and Samael. There is no archangel for Da'at, which is considered to be the dwelling place of The Holy Spirit – called in Hebrew *Ruah ha Kodesh* (the breath of the Holy). The Archangels on the lower part of the Tree will act as your guides in the journey after death, as you gradually move towards the divine throne where you are not judged, but where you review your life and make your own judgement.

The Tree represents the flow of energy between the opposites –

between active and passive, creative and receptive, yang and yin, light and dark, and so on. And so the 12 archangels present us with many contrasting faces: gentle or stern, peaceful or assertive. When you get to know these archangels you will find that some of them call to you more powerfully than others, particularly the one who governs the planet of your zodiac sign, who will be the most important one for you to connect with. You may find one or two of them frightening: if so, this could well be because you are being challenged to work with a new quality in your life. For example, if you find it difficult to be assertive, then you might find Hanael quite threatening, but he is only asking you to stand your own ground and to be strong in life.

In the Jewish tradition the Archangel Metatron watches over the crown at the top of the Tree; he carries a powerful masculine energy and is thought of as a stand-in for God himself. But divine energy in its pure state contains both masculine and feminine qualities, and Metatron has a feminine partner, The Shekinah, or Liberating Angel, sometimes called Rachael or Matrona. The other two archangels above Da'at have a strong parenting quality, especially Raziel, who has a strong fatherly presence, and Zaphkiel, whose energy is similar to Mother Mary or to the Chinese Goddess of Compassion, Kwan Yin. I like to think of this pair as our divine parents.

As the divine energy moves down the Tree it seems to become more feminine or more masculine, according to which side of the Tree it touches. When it arrives at the foot of the Tree, the opposites are reconciled and we once more find two archangels, Sandalphon and Auriel. You will not find Auriel at the gate to the kingdom in traditional Kabbalistic literature, but during my many meditations and inner journeys I have been told that Sandalphon must now have his feminine companion: the kingdom is not complete until there is both a king and a queen. In order for heaven to be brought about on earth, there must be a marriage of masculine and feminine.

When you set out on a mystical journey to meet the archangels on the Tree of Life, you will begin at the foot of the Tree, so I am now going to introduce the archangels to you, beginning with Sandalphon and Auriel, who stand at the first gateway.

SANDALPHON – The Guardian

TRADITIONAL NAME The Messiah
WORKS WELL WITH Ashmodiel,
  Archangel for Taurus

KEYWORDS Trust, Reliability,
  Stewardship
HEAVENLY BODY Earth

Sandalphon represents the divine presence in the kingdom of the created world. He maintains a constant presence within the material reality, which we perceive with our senses, holding the Divine and the material as one.

In a Talmudic story, Moses describes Sandalphon as 'the tall angel': his head reaches to heaven. The mystics tell us that the crown at the top and the kingdom at the bottom are reflections of each other, so the archangels at the top will also be present at the foot. Sandalphon is said to be the twin brother of Metatron, who is at the top of the Tree.

We may picture Sandalphon wearing sandals, walking on our own landscape; he appears as a very physical being, but he towers above us, haloed with colours and vibrations from the cosmic regions. The divine energy is present in every molecule in the created world, in the natural order and in everything humans create as well.

Sandalphon will support you when you wish to create anything of lasting value; he asks you to be considerate and responsible when using natural resources – he is a very ecological archangel! He teaches you how to trust in the goodness and boundless energy of creation and reminds you that you are a divine child.

INVOCATION TO SANDALPHON

Sandalphon, archangel and guardian of this planet I live on, help me to trust in the natural processes of creation, and to be well grounded and responsible in the work I do here. In my daily life I wish to balance the spiritual with the material, I seek only to create harmony and ask you to support me in my efforts.

AURIEL – The Companion

TRADITIONAL NAME The Light of God
WORKS WELL WITH Cael,
  Archangel for Cancer

KEYWORDS Tenderness, Intuition,
  Service
HEAVENLY BODY The Moon

Auriel is an archangel of reflective light and represents the feminine aspect of the Kingdom – she is the bride and Sandalphon the bridegroom. She is the earthly representation of The Shekinah, moving invisibly in creation.

Auriel is the angel of destiny and knows the secrets of our future and our past. Her touch is tender; she is gentle, calling our souls back to her love, like lost sheep to the shepherd. But she is also strong: she is like a lioness when she stands firm to protect her young ones. Her tenderness soothes the troubled heart and reminds us that, while we seek for truth and enlightenment, we should never forget the simple acts of kindness and love – there are so many opportunities for these in every moment of our lives.

Auriel is a mother to the planet earth and all its creatures; she nourishes both the soul and the body. She encourages growth and brings a healing balm to the weak and the lost. She brings dreams and intuitions. Meditate on her when you seek inspiration or wisdom. When Auriel works with Sandalphon they bring balance and harmony into the world. They are both stewards and servants of the kingdom of the Divine.

INVOCATION TO AURIEL

Auriel, archangel and companion, watch over me and nurture me. I am trying to walk a path that is gentle and harmless; please provide me with a guiding light. I need to earn my daily bread while at the same time allowing my spiritual life to develop. I ask you to support me while I learn how to be in the world but not of it.

GABRIEL – The Messenger

TRADITIONAL NAME God is My Strength

WORKS WELL WITH Ambriel, Archangel for Gemini

KEYWORDS Communication, Change, Wakefulness

HEAVENLY BODY Mercury

Gabriel provides a gateway and a bridge between the worlds. He is the first archangel we meet as we journey upwards, whether on the mystical journey or as we move out of our present incarnation at death. He brings messages from heaven down to earth, declaring new inspirations for humanity – the birth of Jesus and the divine word in the Koran. In old frescoes Gabriel kneels before Mary holding up a finger, as if to say 'Pay attention!' and this is also the message he brings to us all. Gabriel asks us to be wakeful and to listen to the voice of the divine deep within our own hearts.

Gabriel brings golden vibrations into the soul, and we translate them, sometimes as music, poetry and dance, sometimes as inspirational messages to open the hearts of our fellow human beings. Not all of us expect to see our name in lights, but working with Gabriel will bring an inner light and you will shine like a star.

Whenever there is change in your life, Gabriel will be there – he is a transitional archangel. He reminds us of the promises we made before we incarnated, and may surprise us with new visions. His messages come in many forms; do not always expect them as dramatic visions, they may well be small signs that you will miss unless you are attentive!

INVOCATION TO GABRIEL

Gabriel, archangel and messenger of divine intelligence, I am open to guidance and ask you to provide me with the information I need for my spiritual journey. I am travelling on a path that sometimes seems winding and complicated; please bring clarity and insight. I am willing to change in order to move forward.

HANAEL – The Warrior

TRADITIONAL NAME Glory of God
WORKS WELL WITH Saraquael,
   Archangel for Aries

KEYWORDS Vitality, Protection,
   Determination
HEAVENLY BODY Mars

Hanael brings new energy and a sense of direction. He never ceases in his intention to assert the life force and to conquer doubt. His energy is vigorous and tenacious; his task is to drive us forward to succeed in our life purpose. Whenever we feel threatened or down at heart, Hanael stirs us into action and provides us with spiritual armour. He encourages us to persevere against the odds, to be brave and determined. With Hanael by our side we have access to the traditional virtues of the knight: valour, dignity and compassion for the weak.

Because Hanael energises us with pure life force, he is a powerful ally when fighting illness, especially those debilitating diseases that drain the patient of energy. He will help you to marshal resistance at all levels – by activating the blood against a physical virus, and also by activating the spiritual force field, which allows us to face the difficulties we meet on our journey.

Hanael also supports us in our creative process, in maintaining our focus on the task in hand so that we can carry it through to the end. Although he is a warrior, Hanael does not wish us to go into unnecessary conflicts, only to be able to stand our ground and to assert our own needs with calm determination.

INVOCATION TO HANAEL

Hanael, archangel and warrior, watch over me and encourage me when I am feeling weak. Help me to assert my own needs without trespassing on the rights of others. I wish to use my drive for creative achievements that will be for the greater good. Please show me how to use my warrior energy for positive and constructive purposes.

RAPHAEL – The Healer

TRADITIONAL NAME Divine Physician
WORKS WELL WITH Zuriel,
   Archangel for Libra

KEYWORDS Balance, Renewal,
   Kindness
HEAVENLY BODY Venus

Raphael brings comfort and healing to all those who are lost on their path. She reassures us and brings us back to harmony and peace when we feel unsettled or perplexed. Her gentle energy always seeks equilibrium and she fills our hearts with new understanding.

Healing of the body is intimately connected with healing of the heart, and Raphael brings both. She helps us to cast out negativity and patiently encourages us to move forward. Her job is to bring in the new by helping us to realign ourselves with our original purpose. She brings people together who can assist in these processes, and is the matchmaker archangel who organises meetings between soulmates.

The beautiful Jewish mystical text, *The Zohar* (The Book of Splendour), tells us that Raphael is also charged with the healing of the earth, so it will be a suitable home for humanity. We must work with her to that end, for healing our planet is a part of healing ourselves.

Raphael has enormous power over demons (remember the story of Tobias?), and when we realise that the demons are created from our negative thought patterns we can work with Raphael to release them. Then we can use the energy for more positive purposes.

INVOCATION TO RAPHAEL

Raphael, archangel and divine healer, I understand that divine love heals all things and I open myself to the flow of this love. I seek healing for myself and the inspiration to heal others I meet. Remind me, day by day, that we are all connected, and help me unblock the channels through which love can flow into my life.

MICHAEL – The Leader

TRADITIONAL NAMES Like unto God, Commander in Chief
WORKS WELL WITH Zerachiel, Archangel for Leo

KEYWORDS Courage, Stability, Sovereignty
HEAVENLY BODY The Sun

Michael is commander of all archangels and provides a stable pivot around which all the others move; he is like an emperor among kings. When we are connected to Michael's energy we have certainty in divine power, and know that all our tasks and spiritual commissions can be completed without effort or anxiety.

When there is no ruler in a land there is no guide, no point of reference, and things become chaotic and uncertain. And in our personal lives we need to understand our central purpose, which comes from our heart; then we can become commanders of our own destiny.

We must also understand that a good sovereign rules the people firmly but gently, and is a facilitator, not a dictator. In this way a ruler becomes a servant, acting in the interests of the community. The divine throne in our hearts provides us with an inner core, so that our other activities become coordinated into a holistic vision based on our heartfelt purpose.

Michael rules the sun, and he brings a golden sunshine into our lives, encouraging us when we are timid and weak. With Michael by your side you will have no fear; he carries a crown of light and a sword of certainty.

INVOCATION TO MICHAEL

Michael, archangel and leader, wise commander over all archangels, open my heart to the true beauty of divine power. Help me to take charge of my own spiritual destiny, and to be the commander of my own life. Allow the centre of divine light, which resides within me, to unfold its radiance and shine in its true splendour.

ZADKIEL – The Comforter

TRADITIONAL NAMES Angel of
Benevolence, The Righteousness of God
WORKS WELL WITH Adnachiel,
Archangel for Sagittarius

KEYWORDS Encouragement,
Generosity, Comfort
HEAVENLY BODY Jupiter

Zadkiel brings us wealth both spiritual and material. He provides a soft place to relax and a haven of comfort after times of adversity. He encourages us on our journey and protects us from our fears. He represents the boundless abundance of our divine parents, and reminds us that it is only our own self-created barriers that keep us from manifesting everything that we need for material abundance and spiritual delight.

When we stumble, Zadkiel picks us up; when we stray from the path, he calls us back. He provides us with our security blanket, cosseting us in divine luxury so that we can relax and be at ease in the world.

We are provided with all the resources we need for our life path. And Zadkiel encourages us to open our own hearts and purses and give freely to others. When we work with Zadkiel we can be confident in the never-ending flow of divine goodness, and we will be able to exchange love and resources without any sense of limitation. Zadkiel does not ration divine abundance, and he does not allow us to count the cost. He asks us to place our trust in the Divine.

INVOCATION TO ZADKIEL

Zadkiel, archangel and comforter, hold my hand as I travel towards my goal. Give me all the things I need in order to move forwards. I know that our divine parents are infinitely generous; help me to open to the boundless abundance of life. Give me the confidence to open my own heart and give generously to others.

SAMAEL – The Administrator

TRADITIONAL NAMES The Adversary, The Tester, Severity of God
WORKS WELL WITH Orphiel, Archangel for Capricorn

KEYWORDS Limitation, Restriction, Discipline
HEAVENLY BODY Saturn

Samael tests our diligence and our dedication. She provides boundaries and limitations in order that we may grow in strength and develop our life purpose. Just as a gardener strips away old wood and dead leaves, Samael takes away anything that is not necessary and reminds us to become focussed and disciplined. We learn best when a stern teacher stands behind us, insisting that we make progress, even when we feel lazy or are inclined to rest on past successes.

Samael is like tempered steel: strong and inflexible, providing the stable girders for our spiritual bridges. Her structures will hold fast against the tempests and earthquakes of our emotional lives. By working with Samael we can lay firm foundations for the creation of an inner city of light, our spiritual home. We only experience difficulties when we resist the divine hand that is pushing us along the true path.

Samael may seem severe, but she is not hard; she only wants the best for her children. We may feel that we have been given tasks that are too difficult, but we are never asked to undertake the impossible. The mountain may seem steep, but we will not be allowed to falter or stumble.

INVOCATION TO SAMAEL

Samael, archangel and administrator, help me to understand the purpose of this testing time. Although your lessons are painful, I realise they provide a learning process and that wisdom is gained through adversity. Encourage me to develop a sense of appropriate limitation, so that I can keep within the boundaries of the true path.

RAZIEL – The Wise; Divine Father

TRADITIONAL NAMES Herald of Deity, Secret of God, Keeper of the Mysteries

WORKS WELL WITH Cambiel, Archangel for Aquarius

KEYWORDS Insight, Perception, Illumination

HEAVENLY BODY Uranus

Raziel is the archangel of the secret regions of creation and chief of the supreme mysteries. He is the author of the legendary *Book of Raziel*, which contains all celestial and earthly knowledge. As our divine father figure he encourages us to discover for ourselves the beauty and intricate complexity of creation. When we gain direct perception of the finest details of the cosmos, we will come face to face with God as Father of all. Then we will realise the part we also play in the unfolding of creation and will know our own divinity.

Raziel is the eye of illumination. He brings a sudden enlightenment, which may startle us if we are not prepared. He makes all things clear and makes transparent everything that was mysterious. We cannot grasp these mysteries with our intellect; we can only understand them in the hidden depths of our own god-consciousness.

When we work with Raziel we must be constantly aware of our responsibility to the rest of creation. We cannot open the book of this precious wisdom and use it for our own gain; if we act destructively in our search for answers we will suffer; and the more we attempt to grasp wisdom, the more it will elude us. Raziel asks us to become enlightened beings, giving our wisdom for the glory of God and the benefit of all.

INVOCATION TO RAZIEL

Raziel, archangel of divine wisdom, like a father you provide me with insight so that I may become an independent and responsible spiritual being. Illuminate the path for me so that I may clearly see the way ahead. Allow me to know the truth with the deepest part of my mind so that I can carry the light with me wherever I go.

ZAPHKIEL – The Compassionate; Divine Mother

TRADITIONAL NAME Contemplation of God

WORKS WELL WITH Barakiel, Archangel for Pisces

KEYWORDS Understanding, Unconditional love, Reconciliation

HEAVENLY BODY Neptune

Zaphkiel is the archangel of divine compassion and unconditional love; like a rose she unfolds her heart to include us all. She heals all our pain and washes our souls in an ocean of boundless love. Her love does not measure us, or ask us to achieve perfection; when we are drawn into her love we discover that we are already perfect.

Zaphkiel offers us grace; she is the cosmic mother who protects and cares for all her children and we are nurtured and blessed in her cradle. Her love is our birthright. When we feel desolate and alone, it is only because we have forgotten how much we are loved; we have closed the shutters on the sunshine, which seeks to warm us. When we open our own hearts we will be amazed at the tenderness that greets us.

When we work with Zaphkiel we will feel a freedom to move in the world as open, loving, spiritual beings, but we will also feel that we are being looked after: when we stumble we are lifted up; when we feel weak we are nurtured and blessed by the ever-flowing grace of the divine mother.

INVOCATION TO ZAPHKIEL

Zaphkiel, archangel of divine compassion, like a mother you cradle me. Encourage me to open my own heart without fear, catch me when I stumble on my path. Allow me to creep back into your arms when I feel weak. I know I am not measured and that you offer unconditional love; help me to give even as I am to receive.

METATRON – The Powerful

TRADITIONAL NAME Angel of the Presence
WORKS WELL WITH Baruel, Archangel for Scorpio

KEYWORDS Judgement, Karma, Transformation
HEAVENLY BODY Pluto

An ancient story tells us that Metatron was once the Prophet Enoch, who was so virtuous that God summoned him to become an archangel. Enoch was transformed in a fire, which consumed his flesh and bones until he became pure spirit and was taken up to the divine throne. This story warns us of the immense power of such an archangel, whose energy is direct, challenging and demanding.

Metatron asks us to live up to very high spiritual standards and to make an unequivocal commitment to whatever task we have chosen for ourselves during this incarnation. When we find ourselves in the presence of Metatron we will undertake our life review, and every secret will be uncovered. During this process we will understand that every action of ours leads inevitably to a chain of reactions, for which we are responsible. All our deeds make up the pattern of our own destiny and we must be very clear when we make choices that they will seriously affect not only our own future but also possibly future generations.

There is no deed, good or bad, so small or insignificant that it is not recorded in the universal Book of Life, and Metatron is the keeper of this book. Metatron will lead you to the true path and when you listen to his voice you will become aware of your own true destiny.

INVOCATION TO METATRON

Metatron, all-powerful judge, I have dedicated myself to a path of transformation and bring my actions into the bright light of your all-seeing eye. I have walked through the darkness and have surrendered all my hopes and desires, seeking to act only in accordance with the divine will. Draw me into the centre and source of all being, so that I may be renewed.

THE SHEKINAH – The Bride; Queen of Heaven

TRADITIONAL NAMES The Liberating Angel, Rachael, Matrona
WORKS WELL WITH Vael, Archangel for Virgo

KEYWORDS Mercy, Communion, Retreat
HEAVENLY BODY Charon (the Moon of Pluto)

The Shekinah is the archangel of liberation because our true freedom lies in complete surrender to the source of life. She demonstrates that our sense of separation, the pain of fragmentation, is an illusion. We live in a shadowland in which it is difficult always to see the Divine at work. But the illusion and the shadowland have been created with our own agreement, in order for us to go on a journey of self-discovery. As humans we are imperfect beings, but when we are at one with our divine parents we realise our own divinity, our own perfection. Then there is no struggle, no alienation, only a sense of completion and wholeness.

Working with The Shekinah involves quiet retreat into meditation or a wordless prayer, which puts us into the timeless place where she resides, waiting to gather us back to the source.

The Shekinah is the archangel of the marriage bed, and she reminds us that in the communion of two people making love we receive an opportunity to experience surrender to the beloved. When we discover that what seemed to be two separate beings are truly one, we receive an opening into the heart of life and understand that we are all one with the Divine, and with all the angels.

INVOCATION TO THE SHEKINAH

Shekinah, merciful face of the Divine, I ask to be reconnected with the source of all life. I know I am a child of the Divine, and all things that seem painful and dark are part of the shadowland in which I live for the time being. Guide me towards wholeness that I may come out of the shadows into the light.

Working with the Archangels of the Tree of Life

Now that you have met all the archangels of the Tree of Life, you can work with them in many ways to bring new possibilities into your life, and the lives of others. You will find it useful to photocopy the diagram on page 162 – get an enlargement if possible. Then you can keep it with you when you journey to meet the archangels.

You should allow plenty of time for all these excursions. And remember, any work you do with such powerful beings will inevitably initiate changes, so you must be prepared to handle what unfolds in your personal life.

Don't forget to write an account of your meetings in your spiritual journal. Here are some suggestions:

ASKING FOR GUIDANCE IN YOUR LIFE

✦ Find out which archangel works well with your zodiac sign. Now take yourself on the inner journey to your sacred building (see page 81) and sit quietly with your guardian angel.

✦ Ask your guardian angel to come with you to visit the archangel you have chosen. In your mind's eye you can move along the paths of the Tree until you come to the right 'gateway'. Imagine you are standing in front of doors that will slide open.

✦ Then speak the archangel's name and ask him to communicate with you. When the doors open, you may be asked inside, or the archangel may come out towards you.

✦ Ask the archangel for guidance for your life at this time.

✦ Then ask him for any necessary spiritual gifts to help you on your way.

✦ Stay with the archangel for as long as you wish, then give thanks and return with your guardian angel to your sacred building.

✦ Remember to bring yourself back along the same route and to ground yourself.

✦ Record your meeting in your journal. You may wish to draw your gift and spend time considering its meaning. The gift may consist of inspirational words – in one of my workshops the Archangel Auriel told one participant 'forgiveness is the fountain of life'. Or you may be offered a symbolic object, such as a sword or a chalice.

Another of my students met Zadkiel behind a 'blue, blue door'. Once in the room and in Zadkiel's presence, he 'was aware of a wonderful rich blue light, but also at the back of it was a radiant white light. I was given a beautiful blue stone and shown how to beam its light-energy to the earth, to heal and bring light. On the way back, the stone dissolved into my heart centre and I felt such love and gratitude.'

A MEETING TO SOLVE PROBLEMS

✦ Before you start this exercise write down a problem that is on your mind.

✦ Now, take a journey to your inner sacred building and sit quietly on your special seat, which is always waiting for you. Ask your guardian angel, your solar archangel and your archangel from the Tree of Life to hold a 'committee meeting' to discuss your problem, and ask them for help.

✦ They may take you elsewhere for this meeting. Allow them to guide you wherever you need to go. Then spend time with them, allowing their energy to surround you. You may not hear the answer directly in words, but you will sense a realignment of your own thinking.

✦ As usual you must bring yourself back, first to your seat in the sacred building, then along the pathways to the garden. Don't forget the grounding.

✦ Write in your journal straight away. Often, you will find that something comes into your mind while you are actually writing, as though you have already been put in touch with the answers but have to write them down in order to realise that they have arrived. I often find that my writing changes while I am doing this kind of exercise, as though the deeper, wiser part of me has been activated.

✦ If you do not feel your problem has been resolved immediately, it is likely that you will suddenly find an answer coming into your mind out of the blue, or that you will have a special and useful dream.

AN INNER JOURNEY THROUGH THE TREE OF LIFE

When you are familiar with the map of the Tree of Life, you can go on inner journeys, starting from the bottom of the Tree, then moving upwards and along the paths, meeting all the archangels as you go. To start with, I suggest you concentrate on the archangels below the circle marked Da'at. The archangels above this space are very powerful and you need to work with the archangels of the lower gateways for a time until you feel quite confident about facing further challenges. You will not be able to meet all these archangels in one sitting. For your first session, start with the lower three, Sandalphon, Auriel and Gabriel.

Take a journey to your sacred building and imagine yourself standing with your guardian angel beside you. Visualise the Tree of Life as a soaring building, with shining gateways on the three pillars. In front of you is the first gateway and here you can ask Sandalphon or Auriel to communicate with you. You should speak to both of them; the order doesn't matter – you may find that both archangels arrive at the same time! Allow time to receive their angelic wisdom and to ask for guidance and help. Then you can acknowledge their help and ask to move up the middle pillar to the next gateway to meet Gabriel. You can imagine yourself being moved upwards using a shining escalator or a lift. When you are in touch with Gabriel, again allow time for a conversation to take place.

When you work with these archangels you may only receive impressions of light, colours or musical sounds. If you do not hear words, please don't worry. The energy of the archangels can move into your whole being at a subtle level and you will experience changes in your life after these visits.

Second session

On the second session you can move quickly past the first three – although you must acknowledge them as you move through the paths – to work with Raphael, Hanael and Michael in exactly the same way as in the first session.

Third session

On your third session you can move quickly past the first six (acknowledging them as you go) to work with Samael and Zadkiel. It is essential to feel positive about your relationship with Samael, the Tester, before moving to visit the archangels beyond Da'at. Samael's energy provides the biggest test for your ego – you must be prepared to work with her to clear your resistance and any negative energy.

Fourth session

✦ When you move through the mysterious space at Da'at, you need to feel as though you are floating free of all your preconceptions. Da'at is like the tunnel of light that appears to people leaving their body in a near-death experience. You could also think of this space as a rainbow bridge. If you imagined the soaring building at the beginning of your journey, then Da'at is an empty floor where there are no escalators or lifts, just your soul's desire to move to a higher realm. This desire will create the means for you to move onwards. You may not 'see' anything, but you will still have your guardian angel beside you.

✦ When you feel ready for the extraordinary power of the archangels at the top of the Tree, allow yourself plenty of quiet time and set up some very strong grounding techniques – have you got a friend who would give you a massage shortly afterwards?

✦ You can approach the archangels above Da'at in exactly the same way as the others, but you should allow separate occasions for Zaphkiel, for Raziel, and then a final one for Metatron and The Shekinah, which is likely to take longer.

All the visits you make to these archangels will be very personal. The only prediction I can make is that your life will undergo changes when you work at this deep level. When you meet the archangels at the top of the Tree, be prepared for some dramatic shifts. By opening yourself to the angels and archangels you are encouraging deep spiritual changes – and this is bound to have a powerful effect on your personal, everyday life.

THE HAMMOCK

This is a very beautiful Tree of Life exercise.

✦ When you are lying in bed at night, preferably flat on your back, imagine you are aligned with the Tree of Life, with Sandalphon and Auriel at your feet, and Metatron and The Shekinah at your crown.

✦ Visualise the archangels at the gates of light as pinpoints, like Christmas tree lights, and the golden threads running between them as strings that make up a hammock beneath you.

✦ Now allow your whole body to sink into the hammock, which supports you in a cradle of light. Breathe deeply and let yourself go . . . Sleep sweetly.

A Farewell Blessing

May your mind be open to the divine
   light that guides you,
May your heart be open to the divine
   love that surrounds you,
May the angels bless you and keep
   you and bring you joy.

APPENDIX
Angelic Symbols

The Renaissance philosophers worked with symbols, which they called *The Writing of the Angels*. There are 23 letters in this angelic writing, each named after one of the letters of the Hebrew alphabet. The letters are made up of pinpoints joined by lines, looking rather like constellations of stars. The old mystics claimed that the writing was inherited from the wisdom of King Solomon, and they used it to open inner gates to higher wisdom.

In 1993 my guides asked me to work with these symbols to channel messages from the angelic realms. I was given a name for each symbol, together with a short message of spiritual wisdom for each symbol and for each archangel on the Tree of Life. I then created a series of visual images for the archangels which my husband Will helped me to develop into a pack of cards that can be used for guidance, or as a focus for meditation (available, with the book of messages, as *The Angels' Script*). Here are ten of the symbols for you to work with. I have included keywords and shortened versions of the messages.

Symbols are useful for spiritual practice because they allow us to work with a powerful concept without using words or complex images. We can easily assimilate simple shapes and take them deep into our awareness, where they can work invisibly to shift our thought patterns. You can work with these symbols during your meditations – you might like to draw them on pieces of paper, using a thick felt pen. Choose a symbol that seems relevant for you at this time, and read the keywords and the message. Then gaze at the symbol for a few moments before closing your eyes and allowing the keywords and the message to penetrate your mind.

Another way to develop your work with symbols is to draw them in the air. This is especially useful when you are feeling in need of protection. The symbol of the Ark, for example, creates a boundary around your aura, which will provide a sense of security.

Beth – The Crucible You are being offered a cup of divine refreshment. This is a gift of health and strength. The chalice of divine love heals your soul and your body and is available to you at all times. Even in times of darkness there is a light waiting to show you the way. You can claim these gifts of love and light whenever you meditate and they will refresh you throughout the day.

Keywords: healing, refreshment, joy, strength, reassurance

Gimel – Delight comes easily into your life and lifts you up when you feel weary. Take time to be playful and to acknowledge that being alive is wonderful. Trust the process of life, and allow it bring you good things. When you express your delight in our wonderful world you bring more joy and happiness into you own life and that of others.

Keywords: playfulness, fun, abundance, harmony, beauty

He – Prayer Allow yourself to surrender to the Divine Spirit, which supports all creation. Offer your own love back to the source, so that your own thoughts go out to all other creatures. Understand the power of pure desire given in humility. You are part of the divine plan and your prayers should be like whispers, saying, 'I do, I do.'

Keywords: humility, reverence, loving care, goodness, creative power

Caph – Fulfilment Your plans and hopes are coming to fruition and you feel as though you have arrived at a destination. Do not expect to stay in this situation for very long, since every arrival is the point of departure for a new stage on your journey. But do take time to recognise how far you have come and learn from any mistakes, so that your path will become smoother in times ahead.

Keywords: conclusion, arrival, evaluation, acknowledgement, rest

Mem – Perfection When you reach a special moment, when everything feels perfect, do not try to freeze the moment or you will block the flow that moves you towards greater things. We cannot say this is perfect or that is perfect, because everything throughout the universe is exactly how it should be, therefore nothing is less than perfect! Allow everything to *be* and you will realise that everything has its own perfection.

Keywords: admiration, recognition, acceptance, wonder, glory

Schin – Hope Even in a dark time we are able to light a candle. From the smallest germ of hope a great ray of divine joy can grow, shining its blessings on everyone. If things have been tough, you may be surprised by a glimpse of light. Then you will realise that angels are everywhere, all the time, even when you do not see them. Open your inner windows and allow the angels into your life.

Keywords: expectation, light, angelic messages, surprise, small steps

Samech – Creativity If you want to create new things in your life, be playful and light in your actions. Focus on your goals but do not hold on too tightly; allow the universal creative energy to support you. Recognise the creative process, from initiation, through growth, then back to the quiet. During the growing time you need to nurture your new possibilities, but always be flexible, allowing things to develop naturally.

Keywords: vision, dedication, commitment, flexibility, awareness

Samach – Wisdom You carry all the wisdom you need for living a fulfilled life. Your wisdom is your inheritance – you are a child of the Divine. This wisdom is in your own heart and you can always turn to it. If you listen to this wisdom you will always make true choices and live in harmony with your own chosen path. You make mistakes only when you forget to listen to your heart.

Keywords: inner knowledge, understanding, conviction, spiritual confidence, divine help

 **Ain – The Ark** Give yourself opportunities for stillness and rest. There is a quiet space in your heart and you need to go there, regularly – not to ask, or to seek for answers, but just to be. You may find there is a physical place – a chapel, or a meditation room – where you can sit quietly. Do not wait with any expectation, but just allow the light of the Divine to open itself in your heart, like a flower.

Keywords: silence, rest, being, waiting, transformation

 **Kuff – Celebration** Find ways to celebrate anything and everything in your life. Do not wait for a birthday or a wedding, and celebrate small things as well as big events. Invite your friends to a party for no reason. Make a magical cake or a pudding and call on your neighbour with some celebration music. Decorate your room with interesting, beautiful or fun things. Dress up in something amazing just because you want to.

Keywords: spontaneity, surprise, dancing, singing, feasting

Resources

Books

Peter Ackroyd, *Blake*, London: Minerva, 1996

Dannion Brinkley with Paul Perry, *Saved by the Light* (introduction by Dr Raymond Moody), London: Piatkus, 1994

Katie Byron, *Loving What Is*, London: Rider, 2002

Deepak Chopra, *How to Know God*, London: Rider, 2000

Theolyn Cortens, *The Angels' Script*, 2nd edition, illustrated by Will Shaman. London: Soul School, 2004. See www.soulschool.co.uk

Alma Daniel, Andrew Ramer and Timothy Wyllie, *Ask Your Angels*, London: Piatkus, 1995

Gustav Davidson, *Dictionary of Angels*, New York: Free Press and London: Collier Macmillan, 1967

Jane Duncan, *Choose Your Thoughts, Change Your Life*, Oxford: Living Well, 1997

Glennyce Eckersley, *Children and Angels*, London: Rider, 1999

Matthew Fox and Rupert Sheldrake, *The Physics of Angels*, San Francisco and New York: Harper, 1996

Rosemary Ellen Guilley, *Angels of Mercy*, New York: Simon and Schuster, 1994

Rosemary Ellen Guilley, *Encyclopaedia of Angels*, New York: Facts on File, 1996

Paul Hawken, *The Magic of Findhorn*, New York and London: Bantam Books, 1976

Emma Heathcote-James, *Seeing Angels*, London: Blake Publishing, 2001

Geoffrey Hodson, *The Brotherhood of Angels and Men*, London: Theosophical Publishing House, 1982

Miranda Holden, *Boundless Love*, London: Rider, 2002

Anne Jones, *Healing Negative Energies*, London: Piatkus 2002

David Lawson, *A Company of Angels*, Forres, Scotland: Findhorn Press, 1998

Dorothy Maclean, *To Hear the Angels Sing*, Forres, Scotland: Findhorn Press, 1981

Dr Raymond Moody, *Life after Life*, New York and London: Bantam Books, 1977

Peter Naylor, *Discovering Dowsing and Divining*, Shire Books. Available from the British Dowsing Society. Tel. 01233 750 253

Elaine Pagels, *The Origin of Satan*, London: Allen Lane, 1996

Martin Palmer, *Living Christianity*, Dorset: Element, 1992

Phyllis V Schlemmer and Palden Jenkins, *The Only Planet of Choice*, Bath: Gateway Books, 1993

David Spangler, *The Laws of Manifestation*, Forres, Scotland: Findhorn Press, 1975 (reprinted until 1981, now out of print)

Eckhardt Tolle, *The Power of Now*, London: Hodder & Stoughton, 1999

Peter Tomkins, *The Secret Life of Nature*, London: Thorsons, 1997

Iyanla Vanzant, *One Day my Soul just Opened Up*, New York: Simon and Schuster, 1998

Neale Donald Walsch, *Conversations with God*, 1, 2, and 3, London: Hodder and Stoughton, 1995, 1997, 1998

Benjamin Woolley, *The Queen's Conjuror: The Science and Magic of Dr Dee*, London: HarperCollins, 2001

Music

This must be a very personal choice – whatever creates the tingle factor for you, but here are some pieces I use in my workshops:

A Feather on the Breath of God, the medieval hymns and sequences of Abbess Hildegarde of Bingen, sung by Gothic Voices, London: Hyperion Records, 1984

Ateh Malkhut, The Harmonic Temple. Four-part chants and canons using sacred texts. Includes one which calls on the four archangels of the directions. Frome, Somerset: Nickomo, Tel. 01373 467324

Laudate Dominum, classical arias and choruses. The soaring voices in Mozart's *Solemn Vespers* take you to heaven! Hayes, Middlesex: EMI Classics For Pleasure, 1988

Bach Lute Suite No. 4 and other pieces, John Williams, London: Sony Essential Classics, 1997

Ave Eva, 12th- and 13th-century songs sung by Brigitte Lesne accompanied by harp. Paris: Opus Productions for the Centre for Mediaeval Music, 1995

Rainforest Reverie, lyrical melodies played on the Japanese Bamboo Flute (*shakuhachi*) by Riley Lee, interwoven with the natural sounds of the rainforest, Suffolk: New World Music, 1993

Self Help Tapes and CDs

Living with Angels visualisations from this book, read by Theolyn with music by Will Shaman. London: Soul School, 2004. See www.soulschool.co.uk

The following tapes and CDs, created by Philip Rogers and Jane Duncan at Living Well, Oxford, are highly recommended. They are not specifically about angels, but are excellent for beginners wanting to meditate, and for anyone who needs to support their self-esteem, or who wants to work on changing negative thought patterns. Philip and Jane are both highly experienced counsellors, who bring great wisdom and integrity to their work. You can contact them by telephone on 0845 458 4050 or through the Living Well website: www.60ways.com

Jane Duncan, *Supporting Your Self Esteem*

Jane Duncan, *Life Supports You*

Jane Duncan, *Making Changes – how to use positive affirmations when you don't believe in them*

Philip Rogers, *The Five Minute Relaxation Tape*

Philip Rogers, *An Introduction to Meditation*

Philip Rogers, *Giving and Receiving Love*

Essences and Remedies

Bach Flower Remedies – widely available, even in general pharmacies

Australian Bush Flower Remedies – also widely available, though usually in dedicated health shops

Angel Rejuvenation Spray – a blend of orchid essences prepared at Machu Picchu with essential oils of frankincense, lavender and geranium. Available from Crescent Moon Direct, tel. 01494 880038 or visit www.crescent-moon.co.uk

Angelic Symbols

The ten angelic symbols in the Appendix are available as pendants. The lines are engraved into polished pewter, which looks like silver, and the dots are tiny crystal fragments; the pendants are delicate and light to wear. They are made by St Justin in Cornwall. They can be ordered through the Soul School website: www.soulschool.co.uk

Websites

www.60ways.com	Website for Jane and Philip Rogers' Living Well publications
www.crescent-moon.co.uk	Suppliers of Angel Rejuvenation Spray and many other delightful gifts, books, videos and music
www.cygnus-books.co.uk	For good books at good prices. Become a free member and receive their monthly magazine
www.emissaryoflight.com	James Twyman's international peace initiative
www.innerbooks.com	Probably the best bookshop for Mind, Body & Spirit in the UK with an excellent second-hand service for out-of-print books and many other bargains. They also do mail order
www.ministryofangels.org.uk	Meeting point for Theolyn Cortens's Ministry of Angels network
www.nickcampion.com	An astrological website
www.soulschool.co.uk	Website of Theolyn Cortens's Soul School educational organisation. A CD of the visualisations in this book is available through this site. Also available are pendants with Angelic symbols (see Appendix). The site also has diary dates for Theolyn's workshops and talks

| www.visionaryliving.com | Rosemary Guilley's website |
| www.worldpuja.com | Project organising synchronised meditations for world peace |

soul school

If you are a spiritual healer, work with Reiki or other energy healing systems, perhaps do channelling work, or would like to develop your spiritual life by working with angels and archangels, you will enjoy Theolyn Cortens's courses.

Theolyn's teaching organisation, Soul School, offers three levels of home-study course – Foundation Level, Advanced Level and a Diploma – for people wishing to teach, or to give spiritual healing and counselling by connecting with angels. Soul School also offers weekend and residential courses and retreats for those wishing to deepen their experience of angels.

To purchase a CD of the guided meditations in this book, or for more information about Theolyn's workshops and home-study courses, please write to: Soul School, PO Box 33873, London N8 9XA and we will send you a prospectus. Or visit the Soul School website at www.soulschool.co.uk

Theolyn has also set up a free-to-join, non-profit organisation called The Ministry of Angels, which aims to create a network of angel groups across the UK. If you are interested in setting up angel groups in your area, to bring more abundance and delight to yourself and to your community, please visit www.ministryofangels.org.uk

Index

Abraham 29
Adnachiel, Archangel 157, 171
affirmations 58–61
alchemy 33, 35
Alister Hardy Research Centre 15n, 50
Ambriel, Archangel 151, 167
'angel of the lord' 29
animals 21, 44, 53, 85, 119, 127
    and zodiac signs 146
Apocrypha, the 133
Aquarius, sign of 146, 149, 168
Aries, sign of 146, 149, 168
ascended masters 21, 44
Ashmodiel, Archangel 150, 165
Ashmolean Museum, Oxford 334
Asmodeus, demon 133
Assyria/ns 27, 29, 72
astrology 28, 33–4, 110, 145–6
    and see zodiac
Augustine, St 122, 123
Auriel, Archangel 16, 75, 76, 91, 131, 152, 178
    and Tree of Life 162, 163, 166, 179, 181
Azrael, Angel of Death 138, 140

Babylon, kingdom of 27, 28, 29, 30, 31
Bailey, Alice 44
Barakiel, Archangel 160, 174
bardo, the 140
Baruel, Archangel 124, 156, 175

Bible, the 3, 10, 27, 37, 38, 114
    angels in 10, 23–4, 27, 28–32, 122
Blake, William 39–40, 62
Blavatsky, Madame Helena Petrovna 43, 50
blessings 67–8, 92–3, 115
    Buddhist 112–13
    farewell 183
    one hundred 92
British Museum 27, 34
Buddhism 3, 76, 112–13
Burne-Jones, Edward 41–2

Caddy, Peter and Eileen 45
Cael, Archangel 124, 152, 166
Cambiel, Archangel 159, 173
Cancer, sign of 124, 152, 166
candles 63, 71, 75, 76, 93, 101
    meditation with 65
Capricorn, sign of 124, 158, 172
Catholicism *see* Roman Catholicism, Roman Catholic Church
Celestial Hierarchies, the 11–12
channelling 6, 52, 73, 74, 86, 185
chanting 56, 74–5, 100
cherubim 7, 11, 12, 28, 95
    descriptions of 23–4, 30
    protection by 114–15
Chesterton, G. K. 60
chi 10, 23
children 52, 92–4, 152

Christianity 3, 10, 11, 15, 16, 27–8, 30, 35, 37
  art of 31, 32
  early 13, 121
  and see Church of England, Protestantism, Reformation, Roman Catholicism, Roman Catholic Church
Church of England 37, 41
co-creating angels
  visualisation for 125, 132
colour/s 16, 17–18, 45, 69
College of Psychic Studies 42
Conan-Doyle, Sir Arthur 44
Cortens, Theolyn
  Discovering Angels 7
  The Angels' Script 6, 52, 102, 185, 191
cosmonauts, Soviet 46–8
Creator, the 9–10, 117
and see God, divine intelligence, Divine Source/Creator
crystals 16, 34, 69, 73, 89, 108, 113–14

Da'at 162, 163, 164, 179, 180
Daniel 31, 141
  Book of 31, 141
death 48, 134, 138–40, 167
  and see near-death experiences
Dee, Dr John 33–6, 37
demons 36, 133, 169
devas 14, 21–2, 44, 46, 97, 109, 150, 154
Devil, the 35, 60, 121–2
divine intelligence 10, 11, 16, 18, 20, 23, 119
Divine Source/Creator 20, 44, 52, 55, 78, 97, 104, 161–2; *and see* God, divine intelligence
Dominions 12

dreams 31, 81, 86, 87, 88–9, 91, 100, 178
dryads 110
Duncan, Philip and Jane 193–4

elementals 21–3, 109–10, 111–14
elements, the: 13–14, 16, 23, 109–10, 111–14, 147
  air 13–14, 16, 22, 110, 112, 147, 151, 155, 159
  earth 13–14, 16, 21–2, 110, 113–14, 147, 150, 154, 158
  fifth 23, 71, 114
  fire 13–14, 15, 16, 22, 110, 111–12, 147, 149, 153, 157
  water 13, 16, 18, 22, 110, 113, 147, 152, 156, 160
Elizabeth I, queen of England 33–4
Enlightenment, the 39
Enoch, Prophet 175
essences 72, 194
Ezekiel, prophet 24, 30

fairies 2, 21–2, 109, 111, 152
Findhorn 22, 45–6, 126
  Angel of 45–6, 117–18, 123
four worlds, the 13, 23, 55, 78, 95, 97, 100, 114, 147
  diagram of 14, 24
  first 14–15, 97, 157
  second 15–18, 55, 97
  third 18–20, 55, 97
  fourth 21–3, 55, 150
  working with 109–14
flowers 63, 71, 119
free will 11, 77

Gabriel, Archangel 16, 31–2, 91, 131, 132, 151
  and William Blake 40

and death 140
and Tree of Life 162, 163, 167, 179
and prophet Muhammed 31
and virgin Mary 18, 31, 167
Garden of Eden 23–4
Geller, Uri 52
Gemini, sign of 151, 167
genies 27
George, St 142
gnomes 22, 113
God 9–10, 34, 39, 56, 67, 97, 114
    and angels 9–10, 28, 34
    biblical 10, 29, 30, 122
    and co-creation 118, 119
    as creator 9–10, 13, 14, 97, 114, 117,
        118
    as divine musician 44
    and Enoch 175
    and 'evil' 121
    love of 14–15
    Raziel and 173
    and Tree of Life 163, 164
    and see Divine Creator/Source,
        divine intelligence
Greece, ancient 10, 113
grounding 79–80, 83, 93, 113, 180
guardian angel/s 7, 18–21, 103, 106,
    123, 177
    discovering your purpose with
        96, 97–100, 101–2
    and the dying 140
    guidance from 78–9, 87–9, 100,
        103, 177–8
    as guide 78–9, 177–8, 180
    meeting 55, 56, 81–5, 87
        visualisation for 81–3
    messages from 87–9

Hardy, Sir Alaster 15n
healers/healing 16, 17, 50, 100–1,
    104, 126, 134–5, 186, 197

angels and 12–13, 131
Raphael and 16, 73, 100–1, 131,
    132–3, 134, 169
Heathcote-James, Emma 49–50,
    192
Hebrew Bible (Old Testament)
    28–9
Hell 35, 121
Henry VIII, king of England 37
hierarchies, celestial 11–12
higher self 21, 57
Hinduism 10, 20, 63
Hodson, Geoffrey: 44–5
    The Brotherhood of Angels and Men
        44–5, 192
    The Coming of the Angels 142
Holy Spirit, the 10
Hughes, Ted 85, 88
humour 60

images 73–4, 107
Immortals, the 10
incense 72, 76
invocations
    to archangels of Tree of Life
        165–76
    to the archangels 76
    to zodiac archangels 149–60
Isaiah, prophet 29
Islam 11, 27–8, 31, 32
Israelites 28–9, 30, 31, 114, 141

Jesus Christ 31, 38, 42, 88, 167
Jewish tradition, the 13, 16, 67, 74,
    91, 92, 114, 117, 121, 146, 161,
    163
    and see Judaism, Kabbalah, Tree
        of Life
Joan of Arc, St 33
Job 122
    Book of 31

journal, spiritual 68, 80–1, 83, 89,
103, 124, 177, 178
Judaism 11, 27–8, 30
and see Jewish tradition
Julian of Norwich, Dame 56

Kabbalah, the 6, 13, 161
and see Tree of Life
karma, 78, 142
Kelley, Edward 34
Koran, the 31, 167
Kwan Yin, goddess 164

Leo, sign of 153, 170
Libra, sign of 155, 169
Lucifer 121, 122
lustral water 72
Luther, Martin 37

Maclean, Dorothy 45–6, 118
To Hear the Angels Sing 118, 192
Man, Isle of 142
manifestation, laws of 126
mantras 63, 64
Marlowe, Christopher 35
Mary, the virgin 18, 31, 164, 167
Matrona 164, 176
meditation 6, 20, 55, 68, 89, 91, 92,
109
on birthdays 148
and co-creation 122, 123, 124,
127
instructions for 63–6
in sacred places 141
and symbols 185
transcendental 3, 62
for world peace 143
Mercury, god 31–2
messages
and angelic symbols 185–6
to angels 106–109

Messiah, the 6, 165
Metatron, Archangel 156, 162, 163,
164, 165, 175, 180, 181
Michael, Archangel 16, 33, 75, 76,
91, 131, 135, 153, 170
and Daniel 31, 141
and England 142
and Tree of Life 162, 163, 179
Michelangelo Buonarotti 40
Middle Ages, the 22, 32, 33
mindfulness 57–61
Ministry of Angels 197
mission statement 102–3
money 104, 105, 125, 126, 135–8
Mons, angels of 42–3
Moody, Dr Raymond 48, 192
Moses 29, 165
Mozart, Wolfgang Amadeus 74,
139, 197
Muhammed, prophet 31
music 74–5, 139, 151, 167, 193

NASA 47–8
nations, archangels of 141–3
nature spirits 2, 7, 21–3, 44, 45,
125–6, 150, 154
meeting 110–14
and see devas, fairies
near-death experiences (NDEs)
48–9, 50, 138, 180
Nebuchadnezzar, king of Babylon
31
New Age, the 36, 44, 50
Newman, John Henry 41
Norway 17, 136
Nostradamus 112

Orphiel, Archangel 124, 158, 172
out-of-body experiences 49–50
Oxford Movement 41

Paul, St 36
pendulum dowsing 89–90, 102
Pisces, sign of 160, 174
places, angels of 141–3
planets, archangels of 147, 149–60
Plato 20
Powers 12
prana 10, 23, 162
prayer/s 11, 42, 56, 66–7, 68, 78, 89, 105, 176
   to the four archangels 91
   St Teresa's 61
   and see invocations
Pre-Raphaelite Brotherhood 41–2
protection 75–6, 114–15, 174
Principalities 12
Protestantism 37–8
Pythagoras 6, 21, 74
Puck 22

Quakerism 38, 45

Rachael 114, 176
Raphael, Archangel 16, 32, 73, 76, 91, 100–1, 114
   and healing 16, 73, 100–1, 131, 132–5, 140, 154
   and Tobias 133–4, 136
Raziel, Archangel 159, 162, 164, 173, 180
   Book of 173
Reformation, the 37–8, 39, 141
Renaissance, the 32, 33, 41, 133, 185
Roman Catholic Church 5, 16, 36–7, 38
Roman Catholicism 5, 41, 87
Rome/Romans, ancient 10, 31–2

sacred space 45, 68–76, 81, 107, 140
Sagittarius, sign of 157, 171
St Patrick's Breastplate 115

salamanders 22, 110, 111
Samael, Archangel 131, 158, 162, 163, 172, 179–80
Sandalphon, Archangel 5–6, 67, 141–2, 150
   and Tree of Life 162, 164, 165, 166, 179, 181
Saraquel, Archangel 6, 102, 149, 168
Satan 31, 121–2
Scorpio, sign of 124, 156, 175
Sefer Yetzirah (Book of Creation) 117
sefiroth 161–3
seraphim, 7, 11, 12, 14–15, 23, 28, 114, 123, 149, 153, 154
   chant of 14, 30, 97, 100
   and fire 14–15, 149
   Isaiah's vision of 30
Shakespeare, William 22, 35
Shaman, Will 5, 7, 185, 191
shefa (the 'everflow') 10–11, 162
Shekinah, The 91, 154, 162, 164, 166, 176, 180, 181
Socrates 97
solar archangel/s 100
   journey to meet 101–2
   working with 100–1, 103, 145, 147–8
Solomon
   King 14, 185
   Song of 3
soul 20, 62, 154
   journey/evolution of 3, 20, 21, 23, 77
   and death 140
soul groups 145, 147, 148
Soul School 197
sound 63, 127–8
   and see music
Spangler, David 126, 192
spirit guides 20, 21
stars 2, 28, 117, 128

Sufis 5, 45, 73, 109
Sun, the 146, 153, 170
Swedenborg, Emanuel 38–9
sylphs 22, 110, 112
symbols 6, 69–71, 79–80, 185–9

talismans 79–80
Talmud, the 123, 165
Taurus, sign of 146, 150, 166
Teresa of Avila, St 36–7, 60–1
theosophy 2–3, 43–5, 142
Theosophical Society 43–4
thought/s
    and co-creation 119–20, 124
    and energy 53, 59–60, 104, 141
    negative 58–9, 120–1, 122, 127, 169
Tibetan bells 75, 76
Tobias 133, 136, 169
Thrones 12
Tree of Life 161–81
    archangels of 6, 7, 161–76
        working with 177–81
    diagram of 162
    journey through 179–80

Uriel, Archangel see Auriel,
    Archangel
undines 22, 110, 113

Vael, Archangel 154, 176
Virgo, sign of 154, 176
Virtues 22

World War, First 42–3
Writing of the Angels, The 6, 185

yoga 63, 65–6, 163

Zadkiel, Archangel 131, 137–8, 157,
    162, 163, 171, 178, 179
Zaphkiel, Archangel 160, 162, 164,
    174, 180
Zerachiel, Archangel 153, 170
zodiac, the 23
    archangels of 6, 145–60, 164, 177
Zuriel, Archangel 155, 169
Zohar, The (The Book of
    Splendour) 169

PIATKUS BOOKS

If you have enjoyed reading this book, you may be interested in other titles published by Piatkus. These include:

0 7499 2293 1	10 Steps to Psychic Power	Cassandra Eason	£12.99
0 7499 2459 4	5-Minute Meditator, The	Eric Harrison	£7.99
0 7499 2160 9	A Woman's Spiritual Journey	Joan Borysenko	£12.99
0 7499 1581 1	At Peace In The Light	Dannion Brinkley	£10.99
0 7499 2062 9	Atlantis Enigma,The	Herbie Brennan	£10.99
0 7499 2129 3	Aura Reading	Cassandra Eason	£8.99
0 7499 2110 2	Balancing Your Chakras	Sonia Choquette	£9.99
0 7499 1981 7	Barefoot Doctor's Handbook For Heroes	Barefoot Doctor	£9.99
0 7499 2201 X	Believing It All	Marc Parent	£9.99
0 7499 1969 8	Book Of Shadows	Phyllis Curott	£10.99
0 7499 1168 9	Care Of The Soul	Thomas Moore	£10.99
0 7499 2019 X	Cassandra Eason's Complete Book Of Tarot	Cassandra Eason	£10.99
0 7499 1763 6	Changes	Soozi Holbeche	£8.99
0 7499 1892 6	Channelling	Lita de Alberdi	£9.99
0 7499 1720 2	Channelling for Everyone	Tony Neate	£10.50
0 7499 1615 X	Child of Eternity, A	A. Rocha and K. Jorde	£12.99
0 7499 1773 3	Children and The Spirit World	Linda Williamson	£8.99
0 7499 1929 9	Chinese Face and Hand Reading	J. O'Brien and M. Palmer	£8.99
0 7499 1824 1	Clear Your Clutter With Feng Shui	Karen Kingston	£7.99
0 7499 2049 1	Colour Healing Manual	Pauline Wills	£12.99
0 7499 1846 2	Colour Your Life	Howard and Dorothy Sun	£10.99
0 7499 2096 3	Colours of the Soul	June McLeod	£10.99
0 7499 2209 5	Complete Book of Women's Wisdom	Cassandra Eason	£10.99

ISBN	Title	Author	Price
0 7499 2304 0	Complete Guide to Divination, A	Cassandra Eason	£7.99
0 7499 2311 3	Complete Guide to Magic and Ritual, The	Cassandra Eason	£7.99
0 7499 2361 X	Complete Guide to Night Magic, The	Cassandra Eason	£9.99
0 7499 2323 7	Compete Guide to Psychic Development	Cassandra Eason	£7.99
0 7499 1596 X	Contacting the Spirit World	Linda Williamson	£10.50
0 7499 1601 X	Creating Sacred Space With Feng Shui	Karen Kingston	£9.99
0 7499 2165 X	Dead Sea Scrolls, The	Stephen Hodge	£10.99
0 7499 2079 3	Dolphin Healing	Horace Dobbs	£10.99
0 7499 2240 0	Encyclopedia of Magic and Ancient Wisdom	Cassandra Eason	£12.99
0 7499 2158 7	Endorphin Effect, The	William Bloom	£12.99
0 7499 2303 2	Energy Healing For Beginners	Ruth White	£9.99
0 7499 1868 3	Essential Nostradamus, The	Peter Lemesurier	£5.99
0 7499 2415 2	Everyday Karma	Carmen Harra	£9.99
0 7499 1927 2	Everyday Rituals and Ceromonies	Lorna St Aubyn	£8.99
0 7499 2145 5	Feng Shui for You and Your Cat	Alison Daniels	£12.99
0 7499 1960 4	Feng Shui Journey, The	Jon Sandifer	£12.99
0 7499 2143 9	Finding Fulfilment	Liz Simpson	£8.99
0 7499 2295 8	Heal Yourself	Anne Jones	£10.99
0 7499 1942 6	Healers and Healing	Roy Stemman	£8.99
0 7499 2308 3	Healing Journey, The	Matthew Manning	£12.99
0 7499 2366 0	Healing Negative Energies	Anne Jones	£10.99
0 7499 2069 6	Healing Power of Light, The	Primrose Cooper	£10.99
0 7499 2109 9	How Meditation Heals	Eric Harrison	£9.99

0 7499 1265 0	I Ching Or Book Of Changes, The	Brian Browne Walker	£7.99
0 7499 2156 0	Jonathan Cainer's Guide To The Zodiac	Jonathan Cainer	£12.99
0 7499 1510 2	Journey of Self Discovery	Ambika Wauters	£8.99
0 7499 2441 1	Joy Diet, The	Martha Beck	£10.99
0 7499 2039 4	Karma and Reincarnation	Ruth White	£9.99
0 7499 1793 8	Lessons of the Lotus	Bhante Y. Wimala	£10.99
0 7499 2137 4	Ley Lines	Danny Sullivan	£9.99
0 7499 2182 X	Life on the Other Side	Sylvia Browne	£12.99
0 7499 1986 8	Light Up Your Life	Diana Cooper	£9.99
0 7499 2247 8	Little Book of Women's Wisdom, The	Judy Ashberg	£4.99
0 7499 2497 7	Living Druidry	Emma Restall Orr	£10.99
0 7499 2071 8	Living Magically	Gill Edwards	£9.99
0 7499 2339 3	Make Your Dreams Come True	Ulli Springett	£9.99
0 7499 1378 9	Many Lives, Many Masters	Brian Weiss	£9.99
0 7499 1958 2	Meditation Plan, The	Richard Lawrence	£10.50
0 7499 2167 6	Messages from the Masters	Brian Weiss	£9.99
0 7499 1422 X	Mindfulness Meditation for Everyday Life	Jon Kabat-Zinn	£10.99
0 7499 2407 1	Modern-Day Druidess, The	Cassandra Eason	£9.99
0 7499 2163 3	Nostradamus in the 21st Century	Peter Lemesurier	£8.99
0 7499 1979 5	One Last Time	John Edward	£9.99
0 7499 2394 6	One-Liners	Ram Dass	£4.99
0 7499 1620 6	Only Love Is Real	Brian Weiss	£9.99
0 7499 2091 2	Other Side and Back, The	Sylvia Browne	£12.99
0 7499 2089 0	Palmistry in the 21st Century	Lori Reid	£8.99
0 7499 2228 1	Past Lives, Future Healing	Sylvia Browne	£12.99
0 7499 1377 0	Past Lives, Present Dreams	Denise Linn	£8.99

0 7499 2392 X	Peace Angels	Antoinette Sampson	£6.99
0 7499 2064 5	Pendulum Dowsing	Cassandra Eason	£7.99
0 7499 2417 9	Piatkus Dictionary of Mind, Body and Spirit	Paula Croxon	£11.99
0 7499 1259 6	Pocketful of Dreams	Denise Linn	£10.99
0 7499 2102 1	Power of Empathy, The	Arthur Ciarimicoli	£10.99
0 7499 1948 5	Power of Inner Peace, The	Diana Cooper	£10.50
0 7499 2422 5	Power of Karma, The	Mary T. Browne	£7.99
0 7499 2238 9	Psyche's Seeds	Jacquelyn Small	£9.99
0 7499 1685 0	Psychic Explorer, The	J. Cainer and C. Rider	£10.99
0 7499 1996 5	Psychic Pathway, The	Sonia Choquette	£9.99
0 7499 2451 9	Psychic Power of Animals, The	Cassandra Eason	£9.99
0 7499 1603 6	Psychic Protection	William Bloom	£8.99
0 7499 2024 6	Psychic World of Derek Acorah, The	Derek Acorah	£9.99
0 7499 2154 4	Pure Bliss	Gill Edwards	£10.99
0 7499 2120 X	Radionics Handbook, The	Keith Mason	£10.99
0 7499 1995 7	Reaching To Heaven	James Van Praagh	£9.99
0 7499 2338 5	Reading the Future	Sasha Fenton	£10.99
0 7499 2066 1	Reiki for Common Ailments	Mari Hall	£12.99
0 7499 2530 2	Reincarnation	Roy Stemman	£7.99
0 7499 2462 4	Ripple Effect, The	Anne Jones	£10.99
0 7499 2233 8	Ruth the Truth's Psychic Guide	Ruth Urquhart	£8.99
0 7499 2196 X	Sacred Healing	Jack and Jan Angelo	£14.99
0 7499 1404 1	Saved By The Light	Dannion Brinkley	£9.99
0 7499 2375 X	Seven Steps to Heaven	Joyce Keller	£9.99
0 7499 1961 2	Soul Purpose	Jackee Holder	£12.99
0 7499 2072 6	Stepping Into The Magic	Gill Edwards	£9.99
0 7499 2321 0	Sylvia Browne's Book Of Dreams	Sylvia Browne	£10.99

0 7499 2246 X	Symbol Therapy	Ulli Springett	£8.99
0 7499 1876 4	Talking To Heaven	James Van Praagh	£9.99
0 7499 1009 7	Tarot Made Easy	Nancy Garen	£12.99
0 7499 1944 2	Transform Your Life	Diana Cooper	£12.99
0 7499 1605 2	Working With Guides and Angels	Ruth White	£8.99
0 7499 1264 2	Working With Your Chakras	Ruth White	£9.99
0 7499 2208 7	Your Shamanic Path	Leo Rutherford	£9.99
0 7499 1903 5	Your Spiritual Journey	Ruth White	£8.99

All Piatkus titles are available from:

Piatkus Books Ltd, c/o Bookpost, PO Box 29, Douglas, Isle of Man, IM99 1BQ

Telephone (+44) 01624 677 237
Fax (+44) 01624 670 923
Email: bookshop@enterprise.net
Free Postage and Packing in the United Kingdom
Credit Cards accepted. All Cheques payable to Bookpost

Prices and availability are subject to change without prior notice. Allow 14 days for delivery. When placing orders, please state if you do not wish to receive any additional information.